MY SUBCONSCIOUSLY
FEMINIST FATHER

MY SUBCONSCIOUSLY FEMINIST FATHER

YASHIKA SINGLA

ALEPH

ALEPH

ALEPH BOOK COMPANY
An independent publishing firm
promoted by *Rupa Publications India*

First published in India in 2023
by Aleph Book Company
7/16 Ansari Road, Daryaganj
New Delhi 110 002

ISBN: 978-93-93852-22-9

1 3 5 7 9 10 8 6 4 2

Printed in India.

For my parents,
for raising three perfectly imperfect humans
(I mostly mean me)!

CONTENTS

INTRODUCTION

I don't remember when I first heard the word *feminism*. It was surely in my adult years when everyone seemed to have different understandings of feminism. There were all sorts of tweaked versions, skewed definitions, and misinterpretations I encountered.

The word feminism perplexes me. It seems to embrace the very conditions it's struggling to break free of: categorizations and stereotypes. I have been told I am a feminist. I don't know if I am, but I do admit I feel extremely deeply about equal respect for all permutations and combinations of chromosomes and I am against sexism at any level in society. I believe in basic respect for everyone's emotions and efforts, for all genders equally. If women can be emotional, men can be too; if men can be tired after two meetings and half a productive day at work, women can too; if husbands can take care of investments, wives can too; and if wives can feed children, husbands must too.

There is a straightforward equation for the abilities and needs of all human beings, over a given timeline of twenty-four hours:

if a = female, b = human being, and c = male,
and $a = b$ and $c = b$,
then $a = c$.

It doesn't matter if they are slightly different in appearance; the net outcome is the same. Going with this explanation, I understand that when a person x believes in the above equation x = feminist. Voila!

I had not read Chimamanda Ngozi Adichie until earlier this year when my sister handed me her book *Dear Ijeawele, or A Feminist Manifesto in Fifteen Suggestions*. I was visiting my sister in the United States, who knew the title was one I wouldn't say no to reading, thereby getting me off her back to let her work in peace. I instantly fell in love with the author and went on to read her other works and listen to her talks on feminism. I loved how she spoke about complex social inequality with such simple yet impactful expressions.

After a couple of videos, I returned to her book. It is a letter to a friend who wants to raise a feminist daughter, and Adichie gives her an almost perfect manifesto for the task. But how often, even in 2023, do mothers really yearn to raise a feminist son? How often do fathers think like that, consciously wanting to raise feminists? I have always wanted to see more feminist sons around me! This string of thoughts inspired me to pick up a pen and paper to write a memoir concerned with equality as the world struggles with the Covid-19 pandemic.

Would it not be nice to see boys and men around us raised to be feminists? Wouldn't that automatically ease the struggles of girls and women, and the tussles between mothers and daughters? They wouldn't have to struggle every day for their basic rights and could work towards their dreams and ambitions. They would be focused on achieving their career goals rather than first trying to get equal rights and respect at home, then fighting for equal respect outside their homes, and *finally* spending their leftover energy in everything else they care about!

While I was considering these thoughts, I started thinking of the reasons that made me feel so strongly about feminism. I realized that I was not the only one thinking so empathetically about feminist issues. My siblings think as I do (that being the only way to identify us as one family, but let's not get into that revelation). Our predilection for equality has more to do with how we were raised by an *ignorant-in-the-matter* father, than it does with the genes our independent and resolute mother passed on to us. It is clearly an acquired trait and not a genotype.

My father accidentally raised three feminists—two daughters and a son—and we've turned out reasonably well (at least the other two did; we are still awaiting my results). My parents have survived the patriarchal society around them without much being sacrificed along the way. I say my father raised feminists accidentally because he really did not know the concept back then nor the consequences of his child-rearing (not that he understands it any better now). If he had had any idea that what he was doing at the time only to be a fair parent would have this impact, he would have definitely made a few corrections, while he had the chance, to his straitjacketed practice of nonconformity to gendered expectations for his children. Together with my mother, he was just trying to raise three children equally: $a = b = c$!

I recently had to move in with my parents for a brief time. It took this year-long vacation at home with my father to realize how similar we are. This similarity is one reason for the conflicts and constant clash of ideas at the dinner table. He is at the age where his diet is restricted, so I have to eat whatever he is allowed to eat. As if eating pumpkins, squashes, gourds, and the like in saltless curries isn't enough of an adjustment, he makes matters worse by discussing topics at the dinner table that give me indigestion. When we are not discussing the plumbing and other home improvement nuisances, we are mostly arguing over how the women around us are treated, especially within Indian society. He tosses out his proud, chauvinistic comments generalizing women, blaming them for their own misery. He knows exactly what to say to trigger me, so he can then have a good laugh and walk away victorious. He loves to see me all worked up and baffled at his clichéd ideologies while I keep attempting rebuttals by giving him examples of his own fairness towards his daughters. It does, however, disappoint him at times to see us all disagreeing with him and that makes me wonder if he really is as patriarchal as he projects or if it is just fun for him to defend that side. He raised me, yes (of course, my mother did too), but he raised me a feminist and now he cannot stand it!

Anyone would think having been raised in India in the eighties and nineties by an independent mother—a full time professor in an all-boys college who sported chic short hair and drove to work in her own car—would be the reason for my brother, sister, and I having grown up to be such strong, independent, feminist individuals. There is no denying that it was our fortune and our privilege, and it has made us what we are today. But my mother did not talk to us about equality, ever. She never sat me down to tell me that I was equal to boys, that I could do everything they were doing, or that she was equal to my father and therefore deserved everything he did. She didn't do anything of the sort. My subconsciously feminist father did.

Extremely stiff, shorter than average for a man, and dressed mostly in formal suits. His rectangular face was framed by a thick, black, squared mane and a heavy black moustache grew under his nose on which rested sharp eyeglasses: this was my father in his child-rearing years. Doc Sa'ab to everyone around, my father always had a serious look on his face, and barely spoke to his children unless necessary. His voice contradicted his petite physique but perfectly matched his personality—loud and scary. Not any more though, now that he is a senior citizen with a few ailments and a couple of surgeries under his belt. He has become softer and more generous with his words and has even developed a sense of humour since he retired (which we've all had a hard time adjusting to).

He is the result of a perfect recipe for an old school, patriarchal dad: born in the forties, in a small, unheard-of town in Punjab, went to a school that taught only in the regional language, became a doctor, and served the government for a good thirty-five or so years. In addition, he served as the chair for healthcare at all important divisions of the state. It's fairly well known that people with great power often tend to have a great sense of self-importance, even leaning towards arrogance. My father is no exception. He is highly judgmental and opinionated about the women *and* men around him and doesn't shy away from saying the meanest things about anyone. If you ask for his opinion, you better be prepared for an uncharitable answer.

My parents fight, just like any other set of parents. They argue incessantly, especially since they have both retired and have nothing better to do with their time. After their morning walk and yoga and spending several hours with the few hundred plants they grow in the house, they are left with plenty of time to argue. It is a part of their daily chores and healthcare routine. I had been staying with them for over a year after a good fifteen years of living on my own and it wasn't easy to live with the childlike versions of my once scary, strict Indian parents, that too in my late thirties.

It took more than three decades and one year of 'reliving' with them to realize that my very proud patriarchal father is actually a subconscious feminist. In fact, it is because of him that I am disturbed by gender inequality in society (as well as by a lot of other herd-mentality social behaviours); it is because of him that I experienced culture shock at the age of twenty-eight in my own country after I married into a different state and culture; it is because of him that I thought moms always drove bigger and better cars than fathers; and it is because of him that I thought only *women* have the right to choose their last names!

I wish everyone had been raised a feminist so that everyone would be as ignorant as I was (in practising sexism), and nobody would know any other way of dealing with issues of gender equality. Raising a feminist is rather easy. It is! If Doc Sa'ab in the eighties could subconsciously raise three children of two genders to be equal, we should definitely give it a try in 2023.

bell hooks rightly said decades ago that feminism is for everybody in her book titled the same, *Feminism Is for Everybody: Passionate Politics*, irrespective of gender, class, religion, or any other socio-economic status that defines a person. Only if we truly understand what feminism means, and realize how simple it really is, can we eliminate the imbalance created by patriarchy. Patriarchy—another heavily loaded word which is often misconstrued as a synonym for sexism—is practised by both men and women who believe that it's the only way to maintain social balance.

That's right. Sexism and patriarchy aren't only practised by men but equally by women in a lot of known or unknown ways—women battling each other for a man's attention; mother-in-law vs daughter-in-law, again a skirmish over a man; and women indulging in sexist jokes or jokes that are derogatory to married women—these are behaviours that fuel the patriarchy and normalize gender inequality. Admiring a bully for a boss because he is a man and calling a woman with an opinion delirious or even the B word is sexism. Therefore, men aren't the only ones who need to learn about feminism, women must understand it too, so that there is not a one-sided defence put forward against the evils of sexism, a common enemy. Feminism is not about angry women who hate men, as some mistakenly understand, nor a bunch of threatened men who hate women.

It isn't about women gaining power over men or lashing out at them. It is not an amorphous design deprived of purpose but a collective scheme that requires constructive application in daily lives for the betterment of all. It is for men as much as it is for women. It is a movement, *together*, against sexism.

I'd like to come back to my father and explain why I am giving him more credit on the subject than you may agree he is entitled to. I wish to share the mistakes he made through my growing up that led to this equalist phenomenon in our family. I call them mistakes because that is what he calls them now, whenever his speeches clash with the beliefs of my siblings and me in arguments at home. He unknowingly instilled in us values that made us misfits in a society that had normalized patriarchy. I am compelled to disseminate what I believe can be the keys to making egalitarianism an easy, unthreatening way of living a life, but only if it is practised by every family as a team. In simple words, I wish to not be a misfit and therefore, wish for more feminist families where all genders are raised to be equalists! I am not a parent and I am no expert at raising anyone, but I do have suggestions based on what worked for my siblings and me.

Having lived in a few different countries and a couple of states with different languages within India, being married for almost a decade, and being an entrepreneur for the same time, I have dealt with enough variety in the last thirty years to conclude that I was undoubtedly lucky to be raised the way I was. I am aware that I hold certain privileges, given that I was born into an upper middle-class family and raised by a dual-income, highly educated, professional couple. However, the female ordeal in the greater fabric of society does not differ much from woman to woman. Thus, it should not detract from the experiences I am about to share.

I have had the fortune of a diverse, multicoloured experience gathered from different cultures. From growing up with my family in Chandigarh to moving to New York at the age of twenty-four; getting married and starting my own architectural firm at twenty-eight in Pune; shedding sweat and blood until the age of thirty-eight for other businesses across the country. I have collected a few experiences and anecdotes that support my claims on prevalent gender biases. These have led me to prepare this unsolicited proclamation of nine suggestions for parents of all genders for raising feminist families. Especially for men raising a son. Please, raise him to be a feminist, and be the hero.

CHAPTER I

NAME TAG

What's in a name? That which we call a rose
By any other name would smell as sweet.

—William Shakespeare, *Romeo and Juliet*

FOR MOST OF MY CHILDHOOD, I attended an all-girls convent school, one of the most prestigious schools in my city. At the beginning of every academic year, we were given planners to note our homework and other important information and dates. The planner had daily prayers and our school anthem, followed by a form with a carbon copy for the school's record and blank, ruled pages. The form was for personal information and it was the most exciting for me to fill in every year. For some unknown reason, it gave me immense pleasure to fill it up in my best handwriting, always better than the entry of the year before.

The form asked for the student's name, her father's name and occupation, her mother's name and occupation, her address, and their phone numbers in addition to other information. On the first day of school, for no particular reason, we looked forward to reading each other's forms. It seemed fun at that time.

In the sixth grade, when we had all just been promoted to the senior block, it felt all the more exciting to be in the new building and to have new books and planners. We must have been between eleven and twelve years old. My friend took my planner and started reading the first personal information page:

Name:	Yashika
Father's Name:	Dr Y. P. Singla
Father's Occupation:	Paediatrician
Mother's Name:	Nirmal Gupta
Mother's Occupation:	Lecturer

She suddenly stopped and looked at me strangely. She asked, 'Why did you write Singla for your father, Gupta for your mother, and no last name for yourself?... Are you adopted?' She laughed.

I told her that those were our names. That did not help take the befuddled expression off her face. 'But if your father's last name is Singla,' she continued, 'your mother's and yours should be Singla, too. Why have you all chosen different names?'

I told her, 'That is my mother's maiden name. Although, you are right that I should have a last name. I will ask my parents why I don't have one.'

She was still confused, 'What do you mean by maiden name? Everyone in a family has the same last name. You can't just write all different names.' She was pensive. 'Is there a serious problem in your family?'

I started laughing. I would probably have taken offence at that last comment now, but I did not understand then what she meant by 'problem in the family'.* I asked her what her parents' original names were. She gave me what would be the expected answer today, although at the time, I did not expect it: 'Mr and Mrs X'. I laughed harder and told her it was funny she did not know her mother's maiden name. It must have been quite a

---

*She was suggesting that my parents might have been separated or divorced.

sight to see two eleven-year-old girls looking at each other in muddled amusement, each thinking the other one was odd.

She had her reasons for thinking my family and I were strange. She immediately grabbed a few planners to demonstrate that, unlike me, everyone else's mother's last name was the same as their father's and how everyone else also had the same last name as both their parents. I had my own reasons for believing *they* were all strange for not knowing that everyone has their own surname, not necessarily the surname of their father or husband (as was the general practice at the time). I thought, if I know the maiden names of my neighbours' mothers, how do these girls in my class not know the maiden names of their own mothers? But I was one against many and I was not very confident in those days. I felt embarrassed because they had all agreed with each other about the surnames and were laughing at me. I felt intimidated and had no way to convince them, or myself, that my family wasn't abnormal. I went home that day with a sense of uneasiness, shrugging my shoulders as I did whenever I was feeling self-conscious or nervous.

I asked my mom that afternoon why her last name was not Singla. She laughed, just like I had laughed earlier in class that day and said, 'Who asked you that?'

She understood that I had not come up with that question on my own. She told me that it was simple. She was already a lecturer when she married my father, and he thought it would be too much trouble to get government documents changed. So, he suggested that she keep her original last name unless she wished to change it. She didn't even have a passport at that time, so I don't know why it would have been so hard for my father to get the name changed.

My father is a conservative Indian man, who takes the meaning of conservative to the next level by also using his time and energy conservatively. This may explain why he wouldn't have wanted to waste his time and energy on the name-change games, and so, told my mother to just be happy with what was given to her by her father. My father was very strict back then, and nobody could argue with him about his decisions. So, my mother had to settle with the name *she* preferred. Simple enough. But why did he not let my siblings and me use a last name? I asked him that same evening.

'You are a child,' he told me. 'You do not understand. It's too much effort changing your passports when you grow up and decide to change surnames. I have kept it blank for all of you so you can decide what surname you want when you grow up.'

Of course, he meant when his daughters grew up and each got married to a man who might keep all his pride and self-respect enclosed in his last name and who would make them adopt his last name and be proud of it, too.

'But then why does everyone else in my class have a last name added everywhere?' I asked.

'They'll wish they didn't, later. You watch!' he said. Then he just laughed and walked away.

I did not understand much that day other than that my father was least enthusiastic when it came to dealing with government offices. That was the only significant discussion I remember having with my parents about our last names. Every now and then, we would receive wedding invitations and New Year's greeting cards addressed to Mr and Mrs Gupta. These were from my mother's colleagues or acquaintances. My father would look at those invitations and call the three of us for a good laugh, pointing out how they were so wrong in writing Mr instead of Dr for him. But *we* had to point out that the last name wasn't even Singla.

'That's okay,' he would casually say. 'They only know your

mom, so they don't know that I go by a different name.'

It was that straightforward. No offence taken. His wife was also a person who had her own set of professional and personal networks and that was OK with him.

I continued through primary school, appeared for India's national entrance exams for engineering, and finished a professional degree in architecture all with just one name. Later, in 2008, I went on to complete my master's degree at Pratt Institute in New York City, also with a single name. My first name: Yashika.

In 1996, Indian American businessman Sabeer Bhatia introduced Hotmail.com. To sign up for an account, I was required to fill out an online form to create a username and password and *that* was the first time I ever had to use my last name. I had to give my last name to complete the form, or it wouldn't go to the next page. My younger brother and I, still in school and very young and enthusiastic, sat down to decide what to put in the last name field. He suggested Gupta, my mother's last name. I told him there was someone with the same name at school, and I did not want myself to be confused with her. With that ingenuous logic, we decided to pick Singla. Yes, that is how my email address got my father's last name!

The second time I was not allowed to go to the next page was in 2008, while I was at Pratt applying for a student visa to attend a summer program in Italy. Italian authorities saw my passport and asked me to prove that Dr Y. P. Singla was indeed my father and that Singla was my last name. They couldn't allow someone with no last name on her passport to enter their country. They told me that my visa to the United States and my Indian government ID were not proof enough of my last name. And they insisted that the passport had to include my last name, and my last name had to be the same as my father's.

That's correct—again the passport! Italy made me go to the Indian consulate in New York to get my last name added to my passport. The Indian consulate obviously refused to cooperate for such a *complicated* matter and told me to travel back to India to get my last name added to my passport. I flew back to India, got my last name added in no time, and applied for an Italian student visa again. Finally, I could go to the next page. Gratitude crept in as I realized I was finally Yashika Singla, without a doubt my father's daughter. No proof needed any more. At last, the passport!

In December 2009, I got married to my best friend from New York and moved to his home state, Maharashtra—new city, new language, and new people. In this new world I had moved to, my last name became the cause of everybody's concern and insomnia. Within a month they started to tell me, one by one, that it was high time I changed my name, *as everyone does*, by taking up my husband's name. Yashika Singla, the name that I did all the gymnastics for, had to be changed. Changed to Yashika + Husband's First Name + Husband's Last Name!

I thought to myself, now wait a minute! Was I supposed to change my name, to have a middle name, to add another set of syllables? A thirty-minute discussion in 1996 with my brother about whether to have my mother's or my father's last name for a Hotmail account was nerve wracking enough. Suddenly, all these strangers were telling me to change it again. To change it to a name I didn't even relate to.

Every time someone suggested this, I would just politely tell them, 'My mother didn't change hers in the 1970s, so why should I change mine in 2010?' To this I would often get either a raised brow, an unamused, or a mistakenly sensible response such as, 'Why did your father allow her?' Surprised again, I would tell them that there was never any permission involved in this. My parents decided mutually. She never asked him if she could keep her last name, and he never decided to be a generous king, entitled to grant such permissions, and allow her that privilege. My father never made it an issue and never projected any authority over my mother's choices of this sort.

Some of my husband's connections, predominantly men, began to call me a rebel and, slowly, words like *stubborn* and *selfish* were applied to me, rarely to my face but often behind my back. I became notorious for being one of *those* girls. All this because I kept my business to myself and did not change my name on my passport—that old antagonist! These name-calling brow raisers were often the kind of men who would be contemptuous of their wives and who would occasionally indulge in wife beating to maintain the power balance in their relationship or to remind their wives of the consequences of questioning male authority.

These were people with professional degrees and with respected qualifications from reputed institutes in India. Some had also lived and worked outside India, seen the world and experienced more progressive societies. Others were raised in cities like Mumbai and Pune, both considered to be more progressive and cosmopolitan than Chandigarh where I was raised. They had diverse social experiences, but their interest in me was the same: was I going to change my name?

A friend of my husband once invited us all to dinner and decided to educate me. She believed that life is a continuous learning curve, one that should only progress upwards with knowledge and experience, and she had plenty to lend. She had lived in different cities in India as an officer's wife. She believed that having a degree in the sciences, an inclination for art, and a profound love for reading self-help books made her the most learned, independent woman I would have had the chance of meeting in my thirty-year-old life. As my personal well-wisher, she told me how strongly she stood by the idea that women should keep their maiden name. In fact, she kept hers for many years because she was a modern woman (just a few years older than me). Until she realized the evils of the practice.

'Oh yes. There are many evils confronting a woman who chooses to keep her maiden name,' she said. She started to list them for me one by one. 'The banks refuse you savings accounts, the income tax department doesn't accept your tax return files, employers have some itch about hiring married women who go by maiden names, stores refuse to show you the sari of your choice, ladies' club parties won't offer you frozen nuggets, deep fried in over-used oil....' The list was endless. That is how inane the conversation sounded to me as she authoritatively rattled on. Of course, I have made up the last few points since I zoned out after the first two and can't remember them all as a result.

I interrupted her droning, 'But Nirmal Gupta buys all the saris she likes and wears them to work!' (That is what I like to believe I interrupted her with at the time.) I then got up from the table to get myself another helping of the lovely dinner she had cooked for us.

My very educated, former New Yorker husband never rescued me nor discussed the name issue whenever it was brought up by his friends and family. He believed that was modern and wise of him. By not discussing the issue, however, he left me to develop my own idea of what he believed on that subject. So, I believed he was on the same page as I was. After all, he was (and still is) amongst the most intelligent and respectful men I've met so far. He believed in equality (so he'd say), and he believed in books. He admired my writing and was the first one to tell me, years ago, that I should write more (he is to blame if readers don't like this book). But he also believed in feminism for the same reason my father believed in patriarchy. To fit in.

Then came a big event in modern India's history. The 2014 elections in India were the largest elections the world had ever seen due to the fact that nearly 814 million people were eligible to vote that year. It was the first time a new government was formed with a majority of any single party since 1984. I was excited to cast my vote in this election since I had been in the United States earlier and missed the previous one. Someone at the local authorities who knew my husband's family had my voter ID made for me. A very thoughtful and generous gesture. The problem was it wasn't in my name. It was Yashika + Husband's First Name + Husband's Last Name. Let's just call the husband Srikhand Bhakri (two sweet and savoury, perfectly nutritious, soft and hard foods, never really eaten together in India, making up metaphorically for a perfect husband name) just to help visualize what my name sounded like every time it was changed without consent. Yashika Singla became Yashika Srikhand Bhakri. I was shocked and upset that this was done without my knowledge, it felt like a passive aggressive way of them telling me, 'This is the identity that we have chosen for you.'

My husband told me I should be grateful for the gesture and not to raise my feminist values again, especially regarding an issue that did not matter much. He said if all I cared about was the right to vote, so why did it matter what name I voted with? But there was another problem. The voter card showed my husband's parents' address as my address. This meant I had to travel 450 kilometres one way just to cast my vote, but I was told that was not a big deal. So, I did travel that distance to cast my vote. But the breaking news next morning didn't contain the headline, 'Girl Battling Identity Crisis Forced to Endure Motion Sickness and Scorching Heat to Travel 450 km to Exercise Voting Rights Like a Good Citizen—Be That Girl!' It would have helped.

I have observed not only in India but also in a few other Western countries that whether to take on a husband's name or not is always a decision involving friction. A married woman's name is the world's concern and how. Another quick story that needs mentioning since it highlights this angelic desire that society, especially Indian society has, to help ignorant women like me is from when I was assaulted in one of the busiest parts of Pune. Though I lived in the city for almost ten years, this was when I was quite new to it. One afternoon while driving, I overtook two men on a slow-moving bike and it offended them. Certainly, it was wrong for a woman driver to overtake two oversized, middle-aged men on a sloppy, slow bike as they changed lanes over and over! They started calling me names in a language that I had not been able to learn as yet, and they accelerated to block my car on the narrow bridge ahead. I rushed to lock my doors and close my windows as they threw stones at my car in rage. That did not get me out of the car, so they started jumping on the tiny eleven-year-old second-hand hatchback that was my ride. In a panic, I called my husband whom I had dropped off at a street corner a couple of minutes ago. In my rear-view mirror, I saw him running to my car with the phone still on his ear. This got the men worried and they ran away before he could reach them, thereby saving me from an action-packed situation witnessed by a thousand entertained onlookers and (a)pathetic passers-by.

We decided to go file a complaint at the closest police station. The police there were very diligent and followed their rules strictly. So, of course, they refused to file my complaint—because I did not have a middle name to write on the complaint form. They questioned if the man accompanying me was even my husband. After all, his name was different from mine. The station officer mocked me for not having a middle name even though not everyone in India has a middle name, especially where I was raised in North India.

I barely ever wrote my last name, only when necessary. But you all know that by now. The officer kept telling others at the station, here is a grown woman who doesn't even know her name. Suddenly, I was a joke, not an assault victim. At that point, I did not know who I was more aggrieved with, the two goons trying to break me into pieces, the police inspectors making the entire complaint about my name, or *my husband* not supporting my argument. Instead he chose to explain the police officers' behaviour in an effort to calm me down (he explained later that he was just trying to wrap things up and get us out of there). After I argued alone with half a dozen men for a good twenty minutes over what the real point was, the inspector decided to be very generous. He told me that helping women in distress was his duty, therefore, he would go ahead and fill out the complaint form on my behalf. He wrote: Complainant: Yashika Srikhand Bhakri. *Sigh*.

A passably irrelevant topic from childhood (in my parents' opinion) had now become a grave issue in my adulthood. It was now the entire world's problem or so it seemed. There was so much done to change my mind and my name. There was so much said that judged my character because of my name. Ironically, wife beaters and cheats and their very victims would all be the first ones to pass judgement. There was such hostility towards the pride I took in my name. The name with which I ran my own architectural firm, which I successfully ran for a decade as an equal partner with my husband. It wasn't just a name I wanted to keep on my social media profiles to vicariously feel like the modern twenty-first-century woman.

Suddenly, the name that my family had given me—the name that reminded me of my father *and* my mother and the ideal childhood I had because of them—was stirring up a hornet's nest everywhere I went. The name either meant so much or so little to my judges that they had stopped discussing the issue and started imposing their opinions. My father never felt challenged or embarrassed by a tiny decision my mother made to choose her original name nor when others questioned him about her choice, which I am sure came in abundance in his time. He did not even flex a muscle, unless it was to laugh, when they addressed him as Mr Gupta on invitations. Did we all not have bigger and more pressing events to attend to in life?

Bit by bit my emotions rose to a clamour. But I sucked them in like a vacuum, down my throat, so I would not make a sound. I lost my will to make noise because I had already made enough over the years, and it had done no good. Making noise didn't even bring me my best friend's support (my husband's), which I'd always assumed was there for me without a doubt. He neither supported nor judged me. He could only understand me as much as his experience allowed. Once again, I was one against many, just like that day in school with the first page in my planner when everyone was laughing at me. However, I told myself there was a silver lining to the situation: although late in life, I had discovered the system of *patriarchy*. Better late than never!

Unsolicited Suggestion #1

It is OK for a woman to keep her maiden name or to take a husband's name or to keep both. Let that be her decision. She might be more inclined to pick a husband's name if not forced to. Sometimes, having been given the choice to decide for oneself is enough for someone to decide in someone else's favour. Choice is enough for someone to become more flexible than they expected of themselves. In any case, *this* last name or *that* last name is more a matter of self-identity than it is a scientific or genetic necessity. Go ahead and debate that all you like.

Dear men, tell yourself and your sons that it is all right if your wife doesn't adopt your name. Tell your friends, tell everyone around you, this is no reason to shame each other. It is no reason to challenge each other's masculinity. Stand up for a woman's choice rather than against it. Her name choice will not change the fact that she is still a wife, nor will it change the human being she is. Choosing your name will not make your wife cook better or earn less than you and it will definitely not make her respect you more.

If your wife doesn't change her last name to yours, it does not mean she is challenging you. Just as choosing your father's name doesn't mean you are challenging your mother or another family member. You are, as a man, living with a name your parents provided. You take utmost pride in it and hold your head up high when it gets recognition professionally or even personally. Why can't your wife, then, have the same feelings?

We are in the twenty-first century, and if a woman still has to struggle with such a trivial issue, we really haven't done our freedom fighters and war heroes any justice. Why should a woman have to defend herself for wanting to keep the name she grew up with, which she believes is her identity? Husbands, how does changing a woman's identity make you a man? Let there be no emotions unnecessarily attached to this decision. For a husband to say, 'It will mean a lot to me and my family if you take my name,' is passive blackmail.

Men, if your wife takes your name in silent acquiescence, please don't convince yourself that it wasn't force or patriarchal pressure, or that it was a decision she made to hold up family values and honour, or that she did it for love. There is no honour and pride in that scenario and *that* certainly is no measure for love.

I am in no way suggesting that women should not adopt their husband's name or that doing so makes her less of a woman. All I wish is for every society to let that decision be nobody's business but that of the woman. Husbands, defend this stance so women won't be slandered for defending their name. Tell your sons and your daughters about their mother's name and her history as much as you would tell them about your own. Let your sons grow up learning *she* is as much a person as *he* is. The hurt and inequality created by enforcing this futile naming tradition on women is doing us no good. It only exemplifies dominance and a need to feel superior to women.

Let's not forget, 'A rose by any other name would smell as sweet.' So, what is all the fuss about? Let the rose be a rose!

CHAPTER 2

GO TEAM!

Teamwork: cooperative or coordinated effort on the part of a group of persons acting together as a team or in the interests of a common cause.

—Dictionary.com

IT IS MY OPINION THAT a family is a group of people related to each other by blood, through marriage, or by mutual commitment. I believe that when a group decides to call themselves a family it makes them a stronger and a more important collection of people, who will watch out for each other's interests with more compassion (presumably). There are families that fall into the traditional patriarchal setup (a man and woman as parents raising children), and there are units that are more equal right from the beginning, successfully overcoming and overriding the patriarchy. These family structures are termed non-traditional.

The traditional and most commonly observed family unit is the one lacking balance the most when it comes to gender equality, therefore, it is the subject of my perusal. There may be no other team more perfect than this team called family, irrespective of its traditional or non-traditional nature. All that needs to be understood is that everything they are trying to achieve in life together has to be dealt with as teamwork. This is how it felt in our house of five. We were a team despite the differences all siblings have and despite not knowing back then that these differences wouldn't necessarily be that despicable in the future!

Most of my childhood was spent in a beautiful neighbourhood in Chandigarh, a city designed for independent India by the French architect Le Corbusier. Ours was a government neighbourhood and it would take living in one to know why I romanticize it so much. It was a perfect storybook setting where I lived for sixteen years, almost until I finished architecture college. Not all city neighbourhoods, even in a perfectly planned city like Chandigarh, break up into quaint streets as pretty and serene as mine. Planted with rows of crimson-leafed kusum trees on either side, this street started in the west from the foothills of the Shivaliks. It reached my neighbourhood via a couple of turns over a few kilometres, giving me the impression that the mountains would travel down to our neighbourhood.

Our house was the third from the left with exposed red brick walls, one of seven lookalikes standing shoulder to shoulder that were mirrored by seven other houses across the street. The wide, lush green gardens in front and behind every duplex were like a soft green carpet, the red brick houses barely visible, peeping from behind the mango, neem, and monkey puzzle trees.

To access the main entrance, visitors had to pass through my makeshift basketball court with its hoop hung just above the huge offensive garage door. The main entrance ushered visitors through a lobby to the most important space in our home: the kitchen. This is where my father could be seen, once a week, washing freshly bought fruits and vegetables in a bright wine-coloured water in big tubs! This was a potassium permanganate solution used to clean all the raw produce from the market. Before they could be eaten, my father had to sort and perfectly align the fruit and vegetables in the refrigerator. He did not trust the domestic help or my mother with this task of picking the right produce and washing it properly. Apparently, there was a right and wrong technique and only he could decide which fruits went on which shelf in the refrigerator, when and how they were cut, and how they were served. Passion!

The rest of the kitchen combat was beyond his comprehension and *therefore*, my mother would take over. He, however, would remind us occasionally that she does it because that is a woman's job, irrespective of whether she is a full-time working woman (in our case). Obviously in an effort to be loyal to societal norms, he would project much chauvinism claiming that *the woman* should cook and serve the family all their daily meals, etcetera. He would be tempted every now and then to cook a few things that he liked to eat for us but would refrain only because of his old school ideas that *that* was her job. Did I not mention he was actively advocating patriarchy but repeatedly failing to practise it? His help in the kitchen with selective chores was against his patriarchal convictions but that did not stop him from contradicting his words with his actions much too often, leaving us all confused about his beliefs and the concept of patriarchy.

My father did all the tasks he did not trust others to do. These included bathing the three of us every day (when we were of the age to be bathed), washing scooters and bicycles, and our two cars every day, watering the front lawns and the extensive kitchen garden in the backyard, and running the fully automatic laundry machine when required. Come to think of it, he really enjoyed playing with water!

We did have some luxuries of living in India. For instance, someone came daily to clean the house and wash the dishes.

But he insisted that everything else was my mom's job. Don't most of us in India still believe it's better if the lady of the house does these things? He did too. The only difference being that he unknowingly divided the labour almost equally between what she did and what he did throughout the week. Teamwork!

His reason for this division of labour was that he thought my mother did not complete those tasks as well as he could. My father is obsessive and compulsive, and this behaviour had a major influence on the emergence of feminism in my house. My mother still believes he was helping her with the house because he *understood* she too went to work the same hours as he did. I don't know where she gets these ideas from.

He could have been a stereotypical Indian man and either not bothered about things that his full-time working wife left unfinished or made a fuss over why those things weren't getting done. He did neither. He was a strict father at home and a senior paediatrician of renown in the city who went on to become Punjab's Deputy Director of Health, but that had nothing to do with his desire for a perfectly managed home even if it meant doing things himself.

The three of us learnt from him that no matter what you are outside the house, no matter what rank you hold in society, no housework is beneath you and doing everything yourself gives you satisfaction and a sense of achievement. I do not remember him ever expecting any praise or applause for this regular work. I even confirmed this observation with my mom. 'I never realized, all these years, that I did not have to thank him for any of this,' she said.

He never wanted a thank you in return for his labour because he never thought he was doing her or anyone else a favour. He was just doing the things that needed to be done in the house—his house. In most homes, these are all additional tasks women do, irrespective of whether they are homemakers or working women. Husbands may cook for their family every Sunday or they may help run the washing machine but they want a pat on the back from their mothers or their wives every time. They phone their mothers and tell them their accomplishments when they help with a single household chore. I don't know what these men were doing growing up, but my brother was polishing everyone's shoes for school every night until they got a glass-like shine, only to get a 'do it better next time' from my father. There were no pats on the back or rewards for doing housework.

When men drop off and pick up their children from school and other places the task becomes laudable. It is called 'spending time with their children'. Wives tell their friends how lucky they are to have a husband who gets the groceries sometimes. Mothers tell their friends that their son, their raja beta—king son, which is what a son is to most Indian mothers, whether they admit it or not—cooks for the daughter-in-law sometimes. Poor him!

Is the house a husband and wife live in not theirs equally? Is it more the wife's or more the husband's? If it is considered a wife's domain, why do the husband and his birth family feel entitled to anything in that house? Also, why do so many women compliment their scrimshanking husbands, compensating for a bad teammate, when he does something out of his pathetic scope of domestic work once in a blue moon? He brings her tea in bed and he becomes her hero!

'He is already doing enough.'

'It's not fair to ask him for more.'

'How can I expect him to do that? He has never done it before. It's unfair to make him do it now.'

'I don't like it done any other way, so I do it myself.'

The list of excuses is endless. Men already have inflated egos and women regularly pump them up by saying all this. How many men say the same about their wives or empathize with them when they have a lot on their plate? This behaviour is a result of the prejudice women have been conditioned to accept year after year. In my experience, even the most modern women think little about this imbalance, which they encourage on a daily basis. Looking after all household chores, fulfilling social commitments on the husband's side, taking care of the elderly in the family if need be, watching after the children and their education or other daily needs—these are just a handful of things that automatically become a woman's prerogative. Women themselves feel guilty if they miss any of these even occasionally or fall sick for a day while the men in their lives wait for the wife/mother to get better and 'take the reins' again. These are men and women raised by mothers who ran the entire house while the fathers dragged their feet!

It is widely understood that for efficient teamwork a team needs to have clear and attainable goals that motivate team members and give them a sense of accomplishment. 'Clear and attainable goals' are seldom a subject of discussion in any household, modern or conventional. This is only a topic of discussion in the workplace. Even if they have the will to share household work, the reason men do not have time for housework—and this is the most common reasoning given regarding labour inequity at home—is because they are busy *earning money*.

The truth is, men are either busy being lazy or busy meeting friends after work, playing a sport, or having *important after-work meetings*. I do not know each and every man, I admit. But I do know enough men who, if not actually doing any of the above activities, are mostly busy covering up for a dear friend who chooses to do everything else except pull his weight at home. In my experience, unlike women, most men often stick together, for each other. They really do. However, women stick together with their family first and with anyone else second.

In 1882, Tarabai Shinde, one of the first feminists and a ferocious one at that, wrote in *Stri Purush Tulana* (A Comparison Between Women and Men) about men during her time:

तुम्हीं एकासाररखे सगलेच दगाबाज, कपटी आहात, तेव्हां तुम्हीं एकमेकांचे झाकून नेतां

(Marathi language written in the Devanagari script)

You are all alike, traitors, hypocrites even, that is why you cover up for each other so well.

I am sure she had her reasons for being so savage. Unfortunately, I've come across many men in the last decade to whom this sentiment can be aptly applied. Isn't it *encouraging* to see how these unhealthy traditions haven't changed much since she wrote that!

Some readers will rush to exclaim, 'not all men are like that!' and I agree, not all men are. I myself have witnessed plenty of good ones as well, but they are hard to find. Let's be honest. The words 'traitor' and 'hypocrite' may be interpreted by the reader as they wish, though their interpretation may well be a reflection of their own personal experiences or guilt.

I tend, compulsively, to see a silver lining in everything. The purpose of quoting Shinde here is not to trigger men or engage in mudslinging, rather it is to highlight how men support each other and have been doing so for centuries. For some reason, this brotherhood is prominent and embedded in society as camaraderie between men much more than there is a sisterhood among women. Whether it is a small lie a husband tells to get away from a social commitment or take rain checks when the wife's family is visiting, or it is a big one that amounts to the level of infidelity; men have got each other's backs. I feel that while women try to develop sisterhood, in most cases, their values and principles often stand in the way of blind support for anyone other than their children. If women had sisterhood embedded in their blood, we would not have the age-old, and still trending, mother-in-law syndrome prevalent in all classes and segments of society.

Even outside of such traditional relationships, women sadly, fall into the trap of constant competition with each other over achievements and prized possessions or overcompensating for their insecurities every time they see another woman doing better. I believe much of these insecurities are fed by internalized sexism. There is no denying that if we decide to lift each other up in solidarity there is no way anything could bring us down. Unfortunately, patriarchy has conditioned us to believe that women need men to feel safe, to survive, and even thrive, therefore, it requires a conscious decision for women to fight for each other and to reach sisterhood.

Men have the superlative ability to support each other as brothers in arms, so why don't they support their wives, partners, and girlfriends? Why don't they support them at home, with their work and their choices? Why don't men support women as a team, before they lose the game?

The modern man wants a woman who is equally educated and qualified, who has spent the same amount of time and money educating herself, who has studied hard like him (if he did at all) to get where she is, and who spends the same time and energy doing paid work as he probably does (probably even more energy given that she faces sexism at work). The modern man's wife is expected, at a bare minimum, to achieve all of these qualifications *and* to take care of the home and her husband's social calls, that he might choose to skip at times (of course, she would be made to feel guilty if *she* skipped). How is that good and balanced teamwork? How are these clear and attainable goals? How will this female team member feel accomplished and motivated?

Tarabai Shinde's original text, in Marathi, has many canonized statements, observations, and apt comparisons of women and men. The passages were translated for me by my ex-best friend, ex-husband, ex-teammate, (Marathi being his mother tongue) as a gesture of support. However, it came too late and after we carelessly lost a fairly easy game. We could have won it, if only he had understood the cardinal rule in time: *be on my side.* Tarabai has written much that is ahead of its time, or maybe, we are drastically behind the times. It pains me to see we have been going around in circles for at least 140 years, if not more.

Tarabai would think that history has gone to waste on us if she came back and saw we are not even halfway to equality yet. We have evolved with time, sure—like a lemon pickle in a jar. The lemon sure changes colour and odour but continues to be a lemon. Life gives us plenty of lemons, why must we give each other more in the name of gender inequality?

Unsolicited Suggestion #2

I cannot stress the importance of being a team and supporting each other as a family enough. If fathers embrace the true meaning of support, do their share of work at home, and not make it seem like a huge favour to help out once in a while, it is sure to make a huge difference.

Dear fathers, please teach your children it is everybody's work, not just the mother's, to keep the house clean. Divide your house chores evenly and save yourself from all the nagging you complain about. I never saw my mother nagging my father or her children. Perhaps that was because everyone was doing their bit. Including my father.

Men, don't compare your wife to your mother. If you do, you should be prepared for comparisons when your wife ends up telling you how her brother or a friend's husband does things better. You will hate it. You might even start hating the person she compared you to. The only person spouses should compare each other to is each other. Let's be clear, comparison doesn't have to be negative. There can be positive comparison, too. Compare who is more overworked, who is getting less sleep, who has had a tougher week at work, and make sure you do everything necessary to make things easier and more equal for each other.

Fathers, be good, be considerate to the person your children love dearly—their mother. Don't think of any work in the house as not manly enough. Everything is your job as much as it is hers. Let your sons grow up with this simple logic, and consequently, you will see how it makes their adult lives less stressful.

Why wait for Mother's Day, birthdays, or your anniversary to give her a special treat or divide household chores? Don't make your wife look forward to such gestures like much-awaited gifts. That would really be a sad life.

Fathers, I believe nothing in this suggestion is a revelation to you. You know this already, but you probably do not understand how much the equal division of unpaid labour and a team spirit at home does to further the cause of feminism. My father shared the household chores with my mother because of a simple logic: it was his house and his duty. Now his son does the same without complaining, and although my father may not be aware of this, the family is secretly proud of raising him a feminist.

CHAPTER 3

WHAT'S YOUR COLOUR?

'Because you are a girl' is never a reason for anything. Ever.

—Chimamanda Ngozi Adichie, *Dear Ijeawele, or*
A Feminist Manifesto in Fifteen Suggestions

MY MOTHER REALIZED MUCH LATER in life that even at the age of four I knew, and very certainly too, what colours and clothes I preferred. She feels bad now for having tortured a child over such a thing. She loved skirts and frocks in her favourite colours, ferozi and fuchsia (I still do not technically know those two colours), and would insist on dressing me in them, especially when we had to go out as a family. I was a placid child, but I threw fits over getting dressed all the time and that surprised and irritated my mother. Until one day, when I was a teenager, she had an epiphany: it wasn't that I did not like dressing up, it was that I had an opinion about what I was made to wear.

All through my too-young-to-communicate years, she would make me wear clothes and colours that made me uncomfortable. Little did she know, I loved only two colours, black and white. That is why I later made her buy me everything in black and white. I was happy in black or white collared shirts (sometimes a checked shirt or two, if I was in an adventurous mood) matched up with big baggy jeans or corduroy pants (fashionable in the nineties) and sporting my basketball shoes or Keds. In her defence, she was just making me wear what my elder sister liked. That one could talk by then and loved (still does) all the pretty things in all the pretty colours that girls are typically expected to like.

Pink is for girls and blue is for boys. This is the most distasteful saying that we hear all too often. Even in popular international TV shows (I won't name names), you see such stereotypes being casually supported. It was all right for my mother in the eighties to not be aware of the concept that colours do not define genders (this lasted for her only until the late eighties), but it's 2023 and we are still thinking this way? As an architect, I have young parents as clients, working professionals, who come to me with a brief of blue walls and blue furniture for their son's room and pink for their daughter's. Most of these couples have children who can barely walk yet. As their consultant, I often tell them they are at a 50 per cent risk that the daughter might grow up to hate them for putting her in a pink *cell* or the son for growing up in that migraine-inducing extra-blue room. They often claim that I am imposing my taste on them! *Me on them!?*

Colours are not the only thing we have assigned to genders. There are so many gender specific stereotypes that are still promoted. Take my proud patriarchal father, for example, who tells his daughter-in-law every now and then that she should start learning to cook now that she is a new mother. Him and his 'women must cook to feed' philosophy! He says this in pungent tones, reminiscent of Tarabai Shinde's strong language. So obviously, a person's first reaction is to revolt. However, if you recap what he said and understand why he said it, you would realize that just like Tarabai, he means it only as a matter of fact. Regarding every task that involved home management and home improvement, our father told all three of us the same thing (irrespective of our gender and our relationship with him) if we balked at our responsibilities. His answer to our resistance was, 'What if you have to live in a jungle one day? You should be prepared.' We would huff and puff and grumble meekly over that bad logic but would still go and do what was asked of us. (I actually did go to live in a kind of a jungle later in life, and his training came in handy.)

My father treated us as three cadets under training in his regiment. Every evening he would return from the hospital and summon us to stand in order by age. Those were some of my earliest safe moments, as I would always be in the centre whether sorted in ascending or descending order, the only time that I felt happy being the middle child. He would then start by scolding us for being bad children, as reported by his chief of staff, my mother, or go directly to assigning our duties for the day. Even if only one was bad on a given day, we would all get court-martialled. It did not matter who did it; we all paid for it.

Ironing clothes for the entire house was one of the trickiest tasks. You needed to know what clothes needed steam and which ones were to be damped and rolled before ironing. Collars were to be ironed first, cuffs should be rolled to iron not flattened or creased, blazers were to have perfectly round shoulders along the seams. My father taught us all of this. Not all clothes go on the hanger, every folded piece should be the same size in the pile, and twenty-seven other trivial details. If I was being punished, I was made to assist him on that job, but on a good day, I would get to do it all by myself with no dagger hanging over my head.

Kanu Priya, the nerdy, perfectionist sister and the eldest sibling who loved make-up and pretty clothes (in addition to theatre and acting), also loved helping in the kitchen. But that would never be her punishment. That was what she loved doing when she took a break from books. On punishment days she would be made to repair all broken gadgets in the house: remote controls, wall clocks, emergency lights, that weird looking carbonated-water machine, the backup iron, the radio set, and anything else that needed her to loosen screws and then tighten them back up. She feared and hated this punishment the most, especially since she knew she could not lose a single screw or mix them up.

Shashaank, the child prodigy and the youngest sibling (a feminist now but pretty mysterious back then) could do nothing right, or so he pretended. That is why I ironically call him the child prodigy. His punishment would be to set the dinner table for everyone (as if that qualified for actual work) and for added value, he would throw in supplementary help for my mom with roti making. He specifically loved to stand there watching over them while they puffed up, then he'd apply ghee and finally, serve us all steaming hot rotis at the table. Wasn't he the most adorable hardworking little brother?

Other less Herculean daily tasks, divided equally amongst us, included assisting with the car wash (you were judged at the end by the amount of water saved in the bucket), hanging out the laundry, picking and folding it when dry, dusting the house, cleaning cupboards every now and then, and whatever other things I like to believe all kids did growing up. Did I make it sound like my father did all this by himself? What are children for if not to be treated as cheap interns? Well, in all honesty, he was preparing us for a self-sufficient jungle life as a backup plan.

The whole point of me airing my dirty childhood laundry is to highlight how no role in my home was assigned on the basis of gender. It was purely on the basis of abilities. The area you lacked in was your punishment task. Simple logic. Dr Singla never ever told us 'because you are a boy' or 'because you are a girl'. Neither did my mom. Well, she watched Bloomberg TV to *relax* and followed the financial markets so she could advise my father on which mutual funds to invest in. She would be the last one to impose gender stereotypes.

I observed people talking about gender roles when I grew up and found them to be the most nonsensical statements ever. I had no concept of *you cannot or should not do it because you are a girl*. Never once did my parents tell me that I was too boyish and should dress up like my sister neither did they tell her that she was too girlish because of the things she liked. They never bought me a doll because I never wanted one. I wanted badminton racquets, basketballs, footballs, roller skates, and a lot of crayons for drawing. They never told my brother that he should be asking for those things instead. All he cared about was recording random television programs on the old VCR and G.I. Joes and Glow Friends in addition to obsessing over Spiderman and Mr India. He did love playing and watching cricket reruns like a maniac (or I should say, like any good Indian). It was the relatives and family friends who would point out these differences and that made my father furious.

Once, after coming home from work, my father saw my sister, barely a teenager then, helping in the kitchen dressed in the traditional salwar kameez (she liked them but seldom wore them). Despite it being a new set, it was ill-fitting.

He reacted rather peculiarly and yelled, 'Why are you in the kitchen and what are you wearing?' 'You will eventually have to wear all this when you grow up,' he told her, 'why do you want to wear them now? In this house, you will not wear all these older-woman clothes nor do I want to see you in the kitchen again.'

In other words, she would definitely be getting married to a sexist husband who would bury her under the sacred load of patriarchy, so she should enjoy her freedom while it lasts! It could be said that he was imposing his ideas on her and forbidding her from doing what she liked—how is that any better than forcing her to do the opposite? Well, I never said he knew what he was doing. That is why I started calling him the *subconsciously feminist father* in the first place! In that house we all had to be discreet with our gender conforming hobbies. Especially Kanu Priya (aka Dr Priya) because on top of those two-dozen other so to speak girly interests, she even liked doing needlework!

As sexist as that may sound, in the twenty-first century unsavoury sexist jokes are making the rounds on social media platforms more than ever before. Everyone loves to share a joke and enjoy a good laugh without giving much thought to what they are actually encouraging. They often even come from women who are putting themselves down. I call it self-sabotage. Two jokes that I've read in 2020 caught my attention—first:

'Be nice to your wife. Restaurants are closed.'

Read during the Covid-19 lockdown; nothing could classify as more recent than that. And the second one:

'A wife asked for a legal opinion from her lawyer husband on why wives are supposed to cook food for their husbands. The husband said, "according to the Geneva Convention all prisoners must be provided with food".'

These are problematic on so many levels. You have to be daft to be still laughing at jokes like these twenty years into the twenty-first century. It is troubling to see that it tickles women to see themselves as someone a husband should be nice to simply because they are the only option for food in the absence of a restaurant, or that husbands are kept prisoner by their wives.

Never had I ever heard my parents or their friends cracking

up at such jokes at their dinners and social gatherings. The first time I started observing such low-lying humour was after I got married and educated young people in our circles would casually crack condescending, sexist jokes. I was expected to laugh, or risk being called a snoot. But I didn't laugh. I could not spot the humour in them. I struggled to hide the extent of my disgust on my face. So, I practised telling myself, 'These people were raised by fluke. Calm down, calm down.'

When a person laughs at a joke like this, they become a part of it, they become party to it, they *become* the joke. I was told I needed to take it easy and not always get so serious, I was too touchy, I needed to learn to laugh (I definitely did not need to learn *that*!). These snides also talked about women drivers as if they had suddenly spotted a flying pig and they are not unique in doing so. The level of indulgent disbelief and mockery when men see a woman parallel park in a tight spot or navigating the highway is astonishing.

I grew up with the mothers around me driving their own cars back and forth to work every day. They are all nearly seventy now and can give any man a run for his money with their uphill slope climbing and parking skills with a stick-shift car, despite poor vision and fragile bones. Then there are men who can't even deal with manual transmissions and flaunt their automatic transmissions (which is all they can handle). The women who are called poor drivers became poor drivers because men have trained them to drive poorly. They are poor drivers because they need to watch out for rash and irresponsible driving in a majority of the streets. No one points out when a man drives poorly!

Women can drive trucks, ride motorbikes, and even fly planes just as well as men do (or as badly in some cases). Like my perplexing father says, 'They only drive better because they are more sensitive to the road than men.' In the same breath

he would say, 'Must be a woman who slowed down the traffic.'
One afternoon last year, we made a bet in continuation of an
argument over the same subject. I think he knew he was on
the losing side, so he started by clearing the air. He stated that
he believed all the women in *his* house drove well, but other
women generally don't.

That afternoon we went on a drive to make a count of
every poor driver, according to *his* judgement alone, within a few
kilometres' radius from home. Within the first twenty minutes,
it was 13:1 men to women, and by the sixth or seventh one,
he had started getting impatient as he was losing yet another
bet with me. In a very sour-grapes defence, he told me I was
being childish to waste his time on such silly things. This is the
same father who till date takes so much pride in his Michael
Schumacher-like skills on Indian roads but loves to sit back and
relax while his daughter-in-law drives him around the city on
a nice day.

Evidently it takes very little to become a feminist—take
small steps, start from home, and all you have to do is believe
in men and women equally!

Unsolicited Suggestion #3

Dear parents, tell your boys, 'Because you are a boy' is never ever a reason for doing or not doing anything. There it is. Said in the most comprehensive and uncomplicated way. Why is it still so hard for us to understand this? If fathers and mothers teach their sons this truth, it will make the lives of girls (and their parents, in fact) a little less complex.

Do you ever wonder who defined gender roles and why do we follow them so blindly even when they lead to sacrifice and unhappiness every single time they are enforced? These roles were defined so long ago that nobody knows for certain how they originated. Just because they have been here forever and you've never questioned or challenged them before, does not mean you cannot challenge them now. How much longer do we have to wait for science and experience to prove to us that there is no real sense in assigning colours to genders or in abiding by gender roles? Have we defined these roles only to suit the privileges of one gender?

In a sense, men are also suppressed because they are made to conform to gender roles. They cannot admit that they are unable to do something because they fear they are not masculine enough if they admit failure. Men, tell your sons it is all right to be weak. Tell them it is all right to say they cannot do something. It is all right to dislike participating in something that all boys do. Tell them it is perfectly OK if they don't like to play sports but enjoy arts and crafts instead. Tell them it is also all right if they want to help their mom in the kitchen rather than watch the game with you.

No job is a man's job or a woman's job. It is simply a job that needs to be done by whoever can do it best. Let your boys understand that. Boys are not girlish if they like baking or if they cry when they are sad, nor are girls boyish if they don't want to wear make-up and like to play football. These ideas are completely senseless. Please don't tell your daughters they are trying too hard if they like driving big cars and don't tell your sons they are sissies if they only want to sit and read books or watch romantic comedies. Talking like this is unintelligent. Consciously discourage such conversations.

My siblings and I did not grow up conforming to these gender roles in our home and that has only made the three of us (and others around us who grew up similarly) better people. This type of rearing doesn't happen without effort. Our upbringing did not confuse us or inhibit our intellectual growth (concerns of those who may defend gender roles). It is plain shameful when child-rearing serves the purpose of oppressing the female sex in the name of society and culture.

Part of the problem, and equally grave, is when a woman says, 'My husband is very liberal. He *lets* me work' or 'How does your husband *allow* you to do this?' It is absurd that men believe women need their permission to work and worse when women believe this too. Women will justify this behaviour by saying, 'I respect my husband, so his decision matters.' Confusing mutual respect with normalization of enforced gender superiority is toxic and self-destructive.

Allow is ascribed to the concept of authority. Governments allow, laws allow, and parents allow their growing children. In my opinion, these are the only three bodies that can allow someone to do something or not. Fathers, tell your sons that it is not for you to *allow* their mother to work or not. It is her choice alone. Make them understand that this *allowing* is the wrong way for two equals to behave.

In Indian society, the husband's family, too, feels entitled to *allow* the daughter-in-law, everything from the kind of clothes she can wear to the people she can meet and whether she can work. This is taking gendered role play to another level all together. The parents already have a son to experiment on and fulfil their parenting goals and passions with. I wonder why most of them still have the uncontrollable desire to foster someone else's adult daughter who's married into their house. If she is qualified enough to be a married woman and to bear children isn't she qualified to decide what clothes to wear and whom to meet?

Dear fathers, tell your sons it is every adult's right to choose if they want to stay home and be a homemaker or go out to work. My mother chose to work before she got married and continued working after. She chose to not take a break when she had three children (she enrolled us in day care to be able to continue working) and at fifty-eight she chose to be at home and not to apply for an extension of retirement. She made all these choices and my overtly patriarchal father never questioned her, discouraged her, or made her feel guilty about them. He only supported her choices.

Tell your sons that when in a relationship with a woman, they should support her, make plans with her, and value and respect her decisions. Make sure they understand that this is what good men do. Good men do not forbid or *allow* women just to 'feel like a man'.

CHAPTER 4

CAREER CHOICE

Nothing in life is to be feared, it is only to be understood.
Now is the time to understand more, so that we may fear less.

—Marie Curie

MADAME CURIE, A LEGEND IN the world of chemistry and physics, has been my idol from the age of eight, when I first read about her in school. What I remember is that one day we read about famous people, and she became my instant favourite because all others were men who looked just the same to an eight-year-old. I read about her again when I was ten and learned she was the first woman to have won the Nobel Prize. In fact, she won it twice in two different sciences, physics and chemistry (both being subjects that I could never get my head around, another one being history). She was an icon for me and I loved to rhetorically ask people, 'Do you think you are Madame Curie?' any time I thought they were acting too smart with me.

I knew there was no way I could become like her because I was not fond of school and academics. I looked forward to rushing home from school to play with my friends in the neighbourhood all afternoon, bossing everyone around (in my sister's words). Kanu Priya read a lot of Linda Goodman as a teenager and told me how I was a perfect Leo girl with natural leadership qualities, well-practised on my gully friends. Things siblings said to each other in the nineties!

My father read none of that, thankfully. He stuck to medical journals but still told me that I would become a boss (he meant I would lead) one day. He said I should choose whatever I wanted but to be sincere, aim for the best, and be at the top in that field. Such vision and confidence for a child who was constantly planning where to play the next game of hide and seek! He had a friend in the Indian Customs Services who would visit us with his family in Chandigarh every summer. He was a tall, square-faced officer of the government's revenue department who wore seamless glasses and dressed neatly in formals. Every time we met, he would greet me with a loud, crisp salute like a subordinate in the police reporting to his officer, 'Good evening, madam.'

He would tell me, 'One day you will become my boss and all my colleagues will line up in their uniforms and salute you like this.'

I never understood why he said that to me, over and over for years. Eventually, *his* wish became one of mine, too. I started dreaming of such success. It made me very nervous because it meant I had to study harder to score well in one of the most difficult entrance tests in the country, conducted by the Union Public Service Commission (UPSC), to become a commissioner in the Indian Revenue Services (IRS). My father's friend wasn't the only one to encourage me to succeed. My father, and occasionally my sister, would join in to tell me I had to get into the IRS. I felt I couldn't let any of them down.

That was a lot of pressure, I will admit, but it gave me immense pleasure to think they thought me capable of it. This was a far better pressure to take on any given day compared to the pressure of 'When you get married, you will know blah

blah blah,' or 'Learn cooking today because it will come in handy when you get married,' or 'We will find you a boy who will be all that glitters.'

No joke. This is what a lot of parents, in one way or another, tell their children, especially daughters. This is institutionalization from a very young age. All this marriage talk and one-day-you'll-have-children talk makes young women and men start thinking about that more than anything else as their final destination.

Believe it or not, the games children play in their formative years leave a lasting impact as much as these gender conditioning conversations around them. Growing up in India, most children play ghar-ghar because a friend, sibling, or parent has passed it on to them and they aspire to play those roles. You do see the problem with this, right? Or maybe not! I, on the other hand, played office-office. I'm not making this up.

Seeing every single parent in my neighbourhood go to the office in the morning and all that boss talk made my friends and I (ten of us with just three girls) come up with this alternate and more fun version of ghar-ghar. We would stack a few cushions on a table and make the highest seat for the boss— the leader, which would be me, and then a second highest seat for my closest friend who played the other boss for that office in the game. The two of us would lead everyone and assign ourselves separate scopes of work to avoid conflict and maintain harmony through the game. Seems like we were both honing our leadership skills at that age! All the other playmates were assigned various posts which were all very respectable titles. But the boys had to take turns to play the *office boy*. I was also amongst the oldest in the group and considered it fair play and none of those seven boys ever objected. Evidently, mine wasn't the only home instilling good values and equality!

I like to believe we were all getting ready to respect women's leadership in adulthood with our unknowing overthrow of patriarchy during these junior school years.

The other boss from our childhood game, one of my closest friends for over three decades to this date, now governs districts in Jammu and Kashmir. She went into the administrative services and chose to serve the most difficult region, geographically, and is doing an inspiring job. A. L. really took the game of office-office and her cushioned-tiered seat to the next level in the real world and is making an impact in more than one way. R. S., the other girl in our career game, was always focused and is now a renowned, award-winning anaesthetist in one of India's most prestigious medical institutes. Everyone else from that team of ten has gone ahead to achieve big and make good lives for themselves. Office-office might not be the reason for all of this, but childhood play definitely plays a part in shaping adults and their dreams.

I too went on to spend a good ten years of my life being *the boss* (I would use the word leader over boss because that is what I relate to being more in all of these situations but it was only after I got into the actual role as a grown up that I understood the difference between the two), leading an architectural firm and a few other small-scale businesses to diversify, including a restaurant. However, this wasn't the career my father or his friend had motivated me to work towards all those years. It was a simple misunderstanding that led me to escape the original plan. I thought cracking the UPSC exam to become an officer with the IRS would be harder than cracking my brain and back for seven years in architecture school (you truly need superhuman powers to get through two different architecture schools)! I do like to believe I was a good leader though—I say leader because *good boss* is a myth, and I don't want to press anyone's buttons.

Ex-employees still call me, even years after moving out of the firm, to wish me well on Teachers' Day. Some tell me they've successfully started their own architectural practices or other businesses and owe it to me. I never know how to react to that but it always fills me with immense gratitude and leaves me feeling that all the back breaking was worth it.

I did not have an exceptional childhood, and I thought everyone around me was growing up being told similar things. As I grew up I realized, to my surprise, that this was not true for children then nor is it true now. Sadly, my childhood was indeed exceptional and not a uniform reality for any socio-economic circle, either in Indian society as a whole or in other cultures around the world, so to speak. I have lived in two countries other than India. I've met and known, intimately, people from a lot of other cultures. Despite our differences, I believe we are all the same. However, this is not always visible to the naked eye.

In all societies, we witness girls being conditioned to the idea of getting married, to accept the responsibility of marriage, and thereafter, childbearing and rearing as their primary and, in many cases, sole responsibility. Some even aspire to and prepare for this traditional role from a very young age. There is nothing wrong with preparing for marriage, but is marriage truly what women should exclusively consider as their end goal? Is marriage really every girl's dream and every girl's ambition? By heavily influencing young women in their formative years with such ideas and examples, are we forcing women's dreams to take the shape of or be replaced by the dreams of patriarchy?

Television, the internet, and other media are not entirely in our control nor are they entirely responsible for sensitizing or desensitizing children today to all sorts of things adults do not approve of. Despite this access to media, it is parents, peers, and community who can make a huge difference in what a young boy or girl is influenced by. Society conveniently blames cinema or the internet for all the wrong that our children are learning. But how often do we realize that children learn by watching the reality around them, by watching *us*, more than by watching fiction. Children are smart enough to recognize fiction and separate it from reality.

In our family home, marriage was a word rarely spoken of, but that is not the case in every Indian household. (The absence of this discussion of marriage has its own set of complexities, but that's beside the point here.) All that was spoken about in our house was career, ambition, and achievement. There was never a question whether you had or would reach any goals or aspirations (just like whether you will get married or not, in most homes), but rather there was an emphasis on what they were. You would think, especially in Indian culture, that this is the most common thing to ask a child: what she or he wants to become when they grow up. Well, that depends on when the child is being asked that question.

We were asked these questions throughout our lives—when we started to speak our first words, as growing children, as teenagers, and as young adults. In my house, these discussions were as vital as discussions of the status of mutual funds and yearly tax returns for my parents. They would make us all sit down and debate our future aspirations when our yearly academic results came out. And the discussions had to be an upgrade from last year based on our performance that year.

Looking at my grades, (and secretly influenced by Bollywood) I once suggested becoming a gangster as one of the obvious career choices. Madame Curie wasn't my only inspiration. I liked wearing clothes like Anil Kapoor wore in most of his movies—half my shirt tucked in and the other half hanging out deliberately, conspiring with my gully gang of ten after school on our plan for the day. To score high enough in school to sit for any entrance tests for college wasn't in my scheme of things until the age of fifteen. Rahul Dravid, the legendary cricketer, inspired me as well. But at that time, it was too late to pick up a sport and make a career of it, so I decided to pick up traits from him instead: aim to excel in whatever you do, be persistent, never be satisfied with your performance, and don't celebrate a victory like it was ultimate or unexpected.

A few too many men directly or indirectly were constantly inspiring me to aim higher and bigger without ever letting me believe that any of the aspirations had to factor in my gender of all the things. Another person who consistently influenced me to aim higher and aspire for better throughout my growing up, was my art teacher Ravindra Sharma, a highly respected artist of national renown. He is from Chandigarh and is a father to three amazing daughters. As my teacher and a friend of the family, he was the one who told me every summer break that I spent time learning to draw and paint from him, that I must become an architect (even though he would call me a birdy fondly because I wanted to fly too or maybe I just looked like one—I never figured!). I didn't know what an architect was at that age, so he told me all about what they did. He was an inspiration for every child who sat there with paper and a few broken crayons. Because of him, I eventually made an honest effort to become an architect. Like I said earlier, I also falsely believed at the time that it was easier than becoming a Revenue Commissioner or more stable a profession than a gangster. Alas!

Having grown up knowing that every woman I met was a working woman, the idea of having a career came rather naturally to me. In my neighbourhood, Mrs L. was a banker, Dr S. a gynaecologist, Mrs K. a professor like my mother, and Mrs V. was a director of education for the state. My mother's

friends were mostly professors and the women who were my
father's friends were all specialists in medicine. For the longest
time, I had no idea how big of a challenge it is to have a career
for most women in the real world outside my tiny social bubble.

In my house, apart from the constant arguments over
everything irrelevant at most times, my parents loved sharing
work gossip. We children would overhear stories about my
mother's college staff—the male clerk who denied her leave,
those male colleagues who never showed up for classes—or
about the Minister of Health (a woman) who, in my father's
words, did 'sterling work' managing such a complex state as
Punjab.

My father told us about the brilliant women in our social
circle and often advised my sister and I that we should yearn
to be *that* remarkable when we grew up. He would talk about
how our school principal was a woman of substance and style
and how we should learn from her to be good administrators.
We were too young to understand any of this, but it stayed
with us until we grew up. It definitely did.

Our principal, Mrs Dutt (fondly referred to as Big Ma'am)
was a woman unlike any I have ever known. She was the principal
of the primary school I attended and I have the fondest memories
of her. This school, single-handedly run and managed by Big
Ma'am, roughly followed the Montessori method of education
and was one of a kind in the eighties. The school was located
in the coziest, most beautiful residential neighbourhood in the
city of Chandigarh. There were sand pits, playgrounds, and
jamun trees; there were poetry recitations under dense gulmohar
trees filled with orange-red flowers; and there was Mistry Ji,
with his open-air carpentry workshop under the neem tree
right in the middle of the campus, smiling behind his cottony
beard, watching everyone bustle about. The school had the

most amazing teachers who left lasting impressions on every child who was fortunate to attend it. The great cricketer Yuvraj Singh would agree.

I was eighteen when I met Big Ma'am again after primary school. She told me, with so much pride, about Yuvraj Singh.

'You remember Yuvraj?' she said. 'That boy is going to make our school very proud. You should go congratulate him when that happens.'

How proud she was of him. Long before he had become the world-renowned cricketer, playing for India and making a mark for himself internationally, she knew he would become famous and be loved globally. (Even though we were just a year apart in school, I did not know Yuvraj well enough, at the time, to go pass on her message to him. I wish I could congratulate him in person now and tell him what she said twenty years ago.)

Big Ma'am was exceptional. She did not fit the stereotypical image of a primary school principal at that time or even now after forty years. Always draped casually in a sari, with carefully stitched sleeveless blouses, her shiny silver hair cut short in a bob, falling on her forehead in the wind, and sporting retro tortoiseshell eyeglasses, Big Ma'am broke all stereotypes. She walked steadily and authoritatively while taking rounds of the campus, an eternally lit cigarette held loosely between her fingers or between her lips when she was not talking. She ran the school like a strict parent, literally raising a few hundred children to excel in books, arts, theatre, and sports, equally, and training the teachers at the same time to become unique exemplary role models. We looked up to her.

Then there were the other teachers: Sylvia Ma'am who made everyone fall in love with her, with her rich perfume, sense of humour, poetry recitations, and goodbye kisses before leaving for home. Raveena Ma'am was prettier than Bollywood and

Hollywood put together. Her high heels left three-inch-deep holes in the soft ground around the entire campus. Both these women were very intelligent and amazing teachers. Sabina Ma'am, whose elocution made everyone want to talk like her, was absolutely elegant. Basically, all of them (including Jasbir Ma'am, Biri Ma'am, Nonu Ma'am, Vij Ma'am, Preeti Ma'am) were beautiful, brilliant women and tremendously important living female inspirations in my most impressionable formative years.

My professor Meta Brunzema, whom I met in New York at the age of twenty-four, was another inspiration for me. She taught me that I could achieve anything if I 'just decided to.' I aspired to be like her, to do so many amazing things in one lifetime, to not be fearful of anything or anyone, and to treat everyone as equal. (That's right! Women do not have to end their life's upward growing curve at the age of twenty-four by rushing to the end goal of getting married by that age.) I only took one class from Meta Brunzema, but even after a decade and a half, she remains a constant motivator for me. In short, there have been numerous women in my life (besides the one who raised me) who have set such high standards for me and women as a whole. My father always pointed them out to me if I ever failed to notice them myself. His constant reminders, giving examples of intelligent and successful women around us was an institutionalization of its own sort—one I would pick any day over the more prevalent kind.

Then came the 2010s when I got married and started noticing just the *opposite* of these role models in abundance, everywhere. These were women from my generation or younger, in Indian metropolitans and cosmopolitans, who had never worked nor seen their mothers work, but would only dream of it. *They dreamt of it?* There were some who worked and considered it their privilege. There were other millennial women who worked full time and thought they were pathbreakers in society. And there were women who worked only because the house needed extra income. I met women who told me how lucky they were to have husbands who understood them enough to 'let them work'. Other women told me, 'you must be doing your businesses as a hobby, since your husband does all the work anyway.' I met all sorts.

There were men, too, who told me their wives didn't like to go out to work, so they supported and encouraged them to stay home (of course I believed them!); men who told me they didn't have a lack of money, so they didn't need to send their wives to work; and men who emphasized that they *allowed* their wives to work. Then there were those men who brought to my notice the extent to which they were progressive: 'I let my wife choose her career, against my own parents' wishes.' Some of them even bought their wives a scooter or a small car to go to work more comfortably. Oh, generous were they, these trailblazers of the twenty-first century, to buy their wife a little ride from her own money.

Interestingly, World Bank's research shows that women are invariably more likely than men to walk or take public transport. Whether it is the eastern countries or the western nations, this fact remains the same around the world. In her book *Invisible Women: Exposing Data Bias in a World Designed for Men*, Caroline Criado Perez states:

> In France, two-thirds of public transport passengers are women; in Philadelphia and Chicago in the US, the figure is 64% and 62% respectively. Meanwhile, men around the world are more likely to drive, and if a household owns a car, it is the men who dominate access to it—even in the feminist utopia that is Sweden.

Perez states another overlooked fact. This uneven distribution is despite the fact that women, almost everywhere, have a more complicated travel pattern than men. Men mostly have to travel between work and home, twice daily in most cases. On the other hand, Perez points out:

> Women do 75% of the world's unpaid care work and this affects their travel needs. A typical female travel pattern involves, for example, dropping children off at school before going to work; taking an elderly relative to the doctor and doing the grocery shopping on the way home. This is called 'trip-chaining,' a travel pattern of several small interconnected trips that has been observed in women around the world.

This underlines my age-old argument that, globally, men *do* display dominance over women by retaining better commuting means for themselves, and women are conditioned to believe that this is a fair arrangement. How?

That was exactly what was happening all around me in that alienating, grown-up world I found myself in. I would think, but what world is this? Why were these women living like this? Why were they sacrificing their comforts and convenience for someone who was not even thinking about them in the first place? Just because they saw other women doing that as well? Why were these men behaving like they were not raised by women, like they didn't know that women need the same comforts? Why were these women wasting their education or even getting educated in fields they had no desire to work in? Why were these men getting married to engineers and women with MBAs and then making them sit at home, with both believing that was normal?

I'm not implying that women should get educated only if

they have a desire to work or that education should only lead to a career. But if some of us actually did get all that education just for *personal growth*, then I am certain that calculus, data circuits, and surface development are really not the kind of personality enhancement topics we were aiming for. There are a dozen other subjects that a woman could study rather than sweating over professional programs in engineering and medicine if they are not going to pursue a career in it, and going ahead for a post-graduation in the same to make matters worse. Could we not try and encourage women instead to read about history so we will at least get acquainted with what women were doing in the past and, perhaps, get some perspective on how so many of them back then were far more progressive than many of us in the present day. Women *and* men should read about women's history so that they become aware and motivated enough to raise a son who isn't just another ignorant and oppressive husband in the future.

A student from my time as an external examiner for a master's degree in urban design in Pune once told me she could not care less for her thesis because she was getting married soon and was planning to have lots of children. I told her she could do both and didn't have to pick one over the other, to which she said, 'My husband's family want a post-graduate for a daughter-in-law but they don't like that I should work because they have a lot of money and a certain status in society.' I did not understand that logic. A master's program can only come after you have completed five years towards a professional degree in architecture, and that is a very expensive program that you really do not need as a minimum qualification for procreation. She wasn't the only student I met with this mindset. Sadly, there are women out there who could not get into a master's program or an engineering college or obtain a degree in medicine because someone else took their place, with no intentions of putting the education to use. Instead, they willingly abandoned their education to the mercy of a future misogynistic husband and his family's oppressive decisions.

I am reminded of the times in Indian theatre and cinema, some hundred-odd years ago, when men played the part of female characters, with their full-grown moustaches (some cared to shave) and hoarse voices. They played women's parts because no story was complete without a woman in it. Isn't it ironic that no woman was allowed to play the part of that very critical female character without whom the story was pointless? Strange paradox.

It was not modern women but rather the women I met as a child and a young adult through my father and mother who were my idols. I aspired to be like my self-made, intelligent mother and like all those other beautiful, successful women who actively applied the education that they acquired. They did not just use their education as a method to earn a living or to qualify for marriage, but to make their own identity regardless of the patriarchy.

Unsolicited Suggestion #4

It is said, 'The way to a man's heart is through his stomach.' Well, so is the way to a woman's heart. Biologically, it is something common to all genders, regardless of the combination of chromosome sets. Cooking is a pretty basic life skill, don't you think? If all their heart desires is a good meal and a full stomach, men can marry a cook, male or female. When are we going to stop using this lame phrase like it is really meaningful? When are we going to stop telling our sons and daughters *this* is the meaning of marriage? Do we really want to teach our daughters that they need to impress men by cooking food for them?

If we insist on having such strange sayings in our languages, I propose adding the following:

The way to a woman's heart is through (believing in) her brain.

The way to a human's heart is through respect.

Or maybe we can just drop this shallow assignment altogether and focus on training our sons and daughters to look at men and women with the same respect. Help them find admiration for a female achiever the same way they idolize a man who has achieved highly in any field. Help them recognize women's achievements other than just their cooking skills. Let them see men and women as humans, not as genders.

Dear parents, don't institutionalize your children to think of marriage as a reward or as an ambition. They listen and adapt everything you say, directly or indirectly. Don't tell your sons you will get them a beautiful wife or tell your daughters they are precious princesses and that you will find them someone who will 'take care of my princess'.

Women are more than just beautiful princesses to their fathers or rewards to husbands. Princesses have also ruled India in ancient history. If you are going to call your daughter a princess, then tell her about Rani Lakshmibai, the legendary warrior who was a symbol of resistance to the British Rule for Indian nationalists in 1857, fearless Razia Sultana, the first female Muslim ruler of the Indian subcontinent in the thirteenth century, or Rani Chennamma, the first female freedom fighter who led an armed force against the British East India Company in 1824, and many others who ruled over parts of India and won wars to protect their kingdoms. Let your *daughter* decide what kind of princess she is. Tell your boys about these fierce women, too, women who protected their own kingdoms and the kingdoms of other men. Tell them these women defeated men in numbers inconceivable. Let them know they can lose to a woman, regardless of being as fierce as the Mughal emperor, Aurangzeb.

Tell your sons about women who are alive today and are making an impact globally. They are all just a click away on the internet. When you start searching, you will realize there is no reason to raise daughters who believe less in themselves or to raise sons with false pride and entitlement. Raising sons to be feminists is as crucial as raising daughters to believe in themselves. Raise a son right and you support a daughter's rights.

Tell your sons to aspire to be a scientist like Ada Lovelace or Rosalind Franklin or an astronaut like Kalpana Chawla. Inspire them to write like Jane Austen or J. K. Rowling or to play tennis like Serena Williams. They are all people who are famous for achieving great things in their respective fields through hard work and commitment. And yes, go ahead and encourage them to pick other people to be their idols, maybe Bill Gates, Ratan Tata, Elon Musk, or even Rafael Nadal. Except, be sure they know not to idolize on the basis of gender but on the basis of achievement and character.

Feminism isn't for women alone to practise. These small steps, as practised by fathers and sons, are small steps towards feminism, towards equality. Feminism isn't always the aggressive activism it has been stereotyped as. It is about actively turning minds against the injustice of oppression; whichever gender is affected. It is to help reduce the unnecessary struggles of the oppressed by simply being more conscious and more human.

Class and culture make a huge impact on the gender-based struggles arising from inequality; thus, they have very different definitions of struggle, but there is no denying that struggle exists. My thoughts and experiences could be applied to all classes because sexism is pretty much the same for a rich man or a poor man—in any country—when it comes to their institutionalization into the practice of gender supremacy and their feelings of superiority over women. I have observed in India specifically, that the middle and lower sections of society have a seemingly sizeable number of double income households where, out of necessity, women are independent financially but remain unaware of the power and strength that comes with that independence in many cases. This is mostly because women themselves don't try to break free from the chains of patriarchy, as it can mean domestic friction and the possibility of stepping into the unchartered territory of independence.

There is still a huge imbalance in the respect given to women in certain classes of society where it is not acknowledged that, in most cases (but especially in lower economic segments), she is also a breadwinner. I believe that a female domestic worker is as much a working woman as the woman she might be working for. In my experience it is common for domestic workers in India to rarely have husbands who are as committed to their jobs or daily wage services as the wives. Perhaps the husbands are content with the woman earning a steady income that they can then indulge in. It's interesting that in certain parts of the world and in large sections of Indian society, this imbalance is observed among all classes, highest to lowest: women work, earn, cook, and raise children. But these women also raise men who only drink, sleep, party, pretend to work, and brag!

Wouldn't it be nice to see these women practising official matriarchy? But we are all institutionalized to believe women are committed to serving and taking care of men, and unless we do that, we are not good women. We also need these men (specifically the kind who make merry at the wife's expense) to be with us only to keep up a sparkling facet of social status that fits the society's definition of a successful household.

In many, so to speak, higher classes and segments of societies (be it in the East or the West), it would not be completely wrong to say there is more gender inequality due to internalized sexist conditioning. In these societies, the real choices for a woman are merely reduced to the choice of the size of a solitaire diamond or a brand of designer clothes or designer furniture, and sometimes, the destination of an international holiday. For some women, being limited to such decisions might be a choice and a source of pleasure, but for many, these limitations are only accepted and normalized for the sake of a family name or some other prideful reason. In many societies, internalized sexism is the real cause for women becoming victims of patriarchy in a way that might actually be irreparable. Men alone cannot bring about the change we are seeking; women must recognize how they are equally contributing to this conditioning.

Men, tell your sons and daughters the difference between a good choice and a bad one but don't deprive them of the experience of *choosing for themselves*. Tell your children that if they let their partner choose something for themselves, it doesn't mean the one getting to make a choice has more power or the other has less. The right of choice is the basic right anyone should have. Tell them and others that just because some women have not had the chance to choose for themselves is not reason enough for them to let their successors be deprived of choice as well. As a man, respect a woman's choice in front of your son, so that he knows the meaning and importance of that choice. Respect a woman's choice in front of another man or a woman so they know it is the normal thing to do. My dear men, take pride in being with a woman who knows what she wants and who knows how to choose a happier life for herself. This, in turn, will only make you and the whole family happier!

CHAPTER 5

FEMINISM BEFOGGED

The male is a biological accident: the y(male) gene is an incomplete x(female) gene, that is, has an incomplete set of chromosomes. In other words, the male is an incomplete female, a walking abortion, aborted at the gene stage.

—Valerie Solanas, *SCUM Manifesto*

SOUNDS EXTREME YOU WOULD SAY. Misandry exists too and nobody addresses that. Isn't that a problem? Misandry exists in the world as much as misogyny does, maybe a little more, some (men) would argue. Misandry exists only as a response to misogyny. Conceivably, women have started becoming hateful towards men in general because men have kept the ingrained oppression and abhorrent prejudices (not to mention exploitation and violence) against women going steady for centuries now. The oppressed were bound to hate the oppressor and revolt someday! That is very valid logic. But who am I to generalize things (based on commonly seen global patterns)? I am not seeking voices to take up arms against this dichotomy, exclaiming 'Not all men!' or 'Not all women!' Yes, not all men. Particularly not a certain kind of man: these men are shining images of the feminist male icon of the twenty-first century, emancipating women since 1982 (or whenever). Nevertheless, what I do know for sure and indisputably so is: misandry is directly proportional to misogyny.

For instance, if we reduce the amount of misogyny in a jar full of men and women, the amount of misandry inside the jar will also reduce in the same proportion (maybe even twice as much given women's generosity). For men to understand this, they should feel free to experiment and see for themselves. If they reduce their prejudices against women, they will see how women start liking them more! Men should not hesitate to perform this experiment at home or in other social environments, making sure to keep children close while executing.

Feminism is a response to this intolerance and these prejudices. It is as much about emancipating men from the prejudices attached to them as it is about women being equal to men. This negative dichotomy—men vs women and women vs men—has caused a lot of confusion and misunderstanding about the real reasons behind feminism and its agenda. Feminism is not about one gender versus the other but about women being equal to men, or women and men as a team of equals.

Then again, there are other kinds of social groups that undermine feminism. One is where men think feminism is a group of women practising hate towards men in keeping with trends. The women of this group do not want to be associated with such *raging women* nor do they really hate men, so instead, they hate feminism and feminists. Another group considers it swag to practise feminism (men and/or women) and think it is all about replacing the cry of 'Equal rights!' with 'Rebel and revolt!' taking the essence of the word *choice* to another level.

Nouveaux Féminists

This latter group, these beguilers of feminism, these nouveau féminist[*] men and women indulge in displays of contempt for traditional morals and values, and *that alone* is the feminist feather in their caps. They talk about feminism more than they rightly practise it. They show off their feminist activism like the nouveau riche show off their money.

I do not judge them completely, like how I won't judge the nouveau riche showing off their money. In a sense, they are helping spread awareness about the need for sexual equality; however, blindly emulating a half-understood idea to gain social popularity can be more a bane than a boon to the movement.

I've heard of a young bureaucrat—twenty something—who was doing great work for one of the state departments. She was intelligent and energetic and was dealing with her public engagement and administrative role with enthusiasm. She wanted to prove women could do as well as or even better than men because, in the past, there had been very few women in that particular department of state affairs in India. She was doing her work most diligently but was still not able to make anyone appreciate or respect her, not just because she was a girl (although that was undoubtedly twice as hard to overcome than any other limitation) but because she would not dress up professionally for her position as was expected of her being an officer of a certain stature. She would wear what she liked and

---

*Nouveaux féminists: author derived word from the expression 'nouveau riche', in this case meaning new feminist. Elaborate meaning for the expression to be found in main text of this chapter. The meaning described in the book is not intended to override or coincide with any other actual meaning for it stated as per the official dictionaries.

mostly be seen chairing that public office in casual clothing, more appropriate for a nineteen or a twenty-year-old college student. It was her choice, she said.

'Why should I wear certain clothes just because I am an officer of the government now? Why should anyone care what I wear to work? This is sexism!' she declared.

But is it sexist to expect a woman to dress up for a professional role, to dress up formally when she holds a respected position, to respect her professional role as much as she expects the institution to respect her in return? If a techie in Silicon Valley went to work all suited up in a tuxedo, it would be the meme of the year. If a Wall Street executive wore a dirty t-shirt, ripped jeans, and old sneakers to the exchange, it would probably bring the stock market down that day. A little exaggeration, sure, but you get the point. It isn't about what she wore or not, it is about what she chose to put up a fight for. For those of us like her who come with certain minimum privileges, it's that simple to forget sometimes, what the fight for equality really means—especially what it means to a lot of underprivileged women out there who just wish they had a job in the first place. Putting up such a misdirected fight by someone in a position that can actually make a difference, does nothing more than distracting everyone from the real problems that are faced by women in workplaces.

Not long ago, I knew a hard-working couple—my peers—with a friendly four-year-old son at the time. They ran their own consultancy firm in Mumbai. They originally came from different towns, Jammu and Meerut—both widely considered conservative towns. With the wife's compassion and hard work and the husband's persistent, unscrupulous networking abilities, they had managed to make a comfortably rich life for themselves in Mumbai. They fit the nouveau riche category perfectly, displaying their new money in all the ways they possibly could to friends and family. The proud wife (of a dissolute husband lacking any real respect for women outside his home) would often brag about how her husband supported her the first time she threw feminism in his family's face.

They got married in his home town, and the day after, she climbed down the magnificent staircase in their family home, overlooking the two dozen, mostly elderly, wedding guests in the main living room. The guests were eagerly waiting to meet the new bride for breakfast. She was wearing a brand-new pair of lounge shorts.

'You should have seen the looks on their faces,' she would laugh.

'I told them proudly, that's my wife,' he added.

'They understood then that I am a modern woman who will not submit to their backwardness,' she continued. '*He* supported me in this by telling me that morning that I should wear shorts to make a statement.'

This woman had grown up wearing quite the contrary in her own parents' house. Perhaps she thought that they didn't need to be subjected to that kind of feminism.

'Oh, I am not like these other small-minded, backward men you have grown up around,' he'd pronounce. 'I am a feminist.' The husband would jump in to add this statement every time they got to narrating the same sagas of nouvelle féminism (over and over). The presumption that he knew what kind of men 'I grew up around' was a healthy dose of his overcompensating self-esteem.

He was right though, in saying that he was not like other men. He would never objectify women, when his wife was around. He limited himself to only passing sleazy, sexist remarks about *other* men's wives in her presence. Of course, she was modern herself, so she encouraged his sense of humour without being judgmental or offended. He respected his wife enough to not disturb her peace with his own tales of indulgent infidelity, but because she was also his best friend, he would never hide from her what was going on in other people's lives. And that was how they kept their trusting relationship going. They liked believing they were unique, modern torchbearers of some sort, but unfortunately, they were just like the abundant nouveau féminist peers present around us. Wouldn't they be happy if they all found each other!

A wise-woman character on television (played by Maggie Smith) once said, 'Vulgarity is no substitute for wit.'* I can't think of a better aphorism than that. Since when did rebelling like a raging pubescent teenager become a pride-worthy display of virtue for men and women? Since when did showing disrespect to our elders or passing off disparaging remarks about other women and calling it harmless humour become the reflection of feminism in any society or culture? And I shudder to think these nouveaux féminists are raising sons.

This is exactly the point where I am unsure of what my parents (and the few other parents I grew up around) did right to prevent their son from becoming a cheap-humoured sexist and my sister and I from becoming passive patrons of such normalized idiocy. Thank God my nouveaux féminists friends did not have Dr Singla watching them every step of the way growing up. He would have court-martialled them and handed them half a bucket of water to wash the car every day for the rest of their childhood lives before they could step into an exemplary adulthood.

---

*The phrase is from *Downton Abbey*, a British historical drama television series set in the early twentieth century.

The other less consciously contradictory (but still warped) form of the nouveaux féminists are the *haters*—lesbian-hating straight women, straight-woman-hating lesbians, men-hating women, and women who advocate infidelity because men do it, etc., etc. We all have rage, and we all have suffered the evils of patriarchy, but is this form of feminism really the kind of equality we are seeking for all women? For some, the ideal feminism might be the much-awaited empathy required for emancipating women who fall in a certain circle of privilege. I fell in one such privileged group, where I thought equal acceptance of women who drink and smoke regularly was the only missing equality in the Indian society. Then there are those who discuss adultery as a choice (since men do it), not realizing they are privileged to have that as one of their primary concerns! But for most others, gender equality is still the fight for basic rights and equal respect in society, equal dignity at work, and equal opportunity to pick a career of preference.

Justifying immorality, hatred, or petty feuding by saying these behaviours are 'my right to choose' is *not* what women of the past hundred or more years have given their lives fighting for. Are we really doing ourselves or other women justice by selfishly stealing the light from the real problems and their causes? For instance, are we not aware of the time men take to process and act on a small request to change a light bulb? Now imagine, on top of their procrastination, you yell in their faces, 'Do not bring the clear glass bulb like last time, I need the semi-frosted, warm white bulb from the lower box on the right side, second shelf from the top, and make sure you pick from the ones put at the bottom to be used first.' Phew! Is that job ever going to get done?

Alright. That was sexist. Guilty as charged. But do you get the point I am trying to make? Women have come so far and gotten ourselves so confused about what we really want from society and from men in the name of feminism, that our struggle has lost its meaning—seems ignoble to some, even— and has yielded little or no real progress in a long time. The common belief amongst many is that feminism means women are better than men or that feminists hate men, or that it is a movement against all men. These are all the major arguments that you hear the minute anyone in a living room uses the word feminism these days. Misinformation and confusion results in people jumping the gun with this kind of defence and being prejudiced against any discussion about basic equality. So, what I'm suggesting is for people to go back to the beginning to reassess their approach to feminism. But this time,

- be patient,
- be more precise about what qualifies as oppression in society,
- give men—and society—a smaller, carefully selected bullet list for expected change,
- pick the most important women's rights-oriented battles in descending order of urgency, and finally,
- start from home. Start by changing how fathers and mothers are raising sons before expecting society itself to change.

Disguised Feminism

Another baffling version of feminism I came across in the last decade is a kind of disguised feminism for the lack of a better term. It has taken me many years of discussions, debates, readings, and a constant search for answers, that included going back and forth between sites of personal experiences, to understand that this societal equality and respect for women was actually a Machiavellian sibling of feminism. This sibling gave the *impression* of gender equality in the well-read and well-fed societies I lived in.

I have spent almost a third of my life in southwestern parts of India (Maharashtra and Goa, mostly), with Maharashtra having a higher male to female ratio and a much higher literacy rate for women compared to most other states in the country. For centuries in India, especially in Maharashtra, women have had the right to education, and even today, in the smallest towns in these parts of the country, there will be more women who have completed their higher education than in other regions of India. The first female physician, Anandi Gopal Joshi, the fierce author Tarabai Shinde, the unparalleled warrior Rani Lakshmibai, the builder of Hindu temples Queen Ahilyabai Holkar, and many other eminent women were all icons from around this region. However, what utterly confuses me is the fact that despite having these historical role models and the right to education and encouragement to continue it even after getting married, most of the women in my circles, whether living in big cities like Pune or Bombay or in the smaller towns of Maharashtra, were either denied the right to work or would reluctantly agree to decline its prospects for the sake of tradition.

I realized the right to work was still a far-fetched ambition after I discovered that women in most households did not even have the right to sit in the same living room as men or even eat before the men of the house did. Whether it was a daily meal or a house party, women gathered to eat at the end of the meal after the men were finished eating. Even at weddings, women and men had separate seating, and this was unseen and unheard of by me, coming from Chandigarh. These women were engineers and MBAs, some had master's degrees in the arts and sciences. My professional experience was contrary to this imbalance and inequality of social status for women in southwest India, where I worked for almost ten years as a business owner. It rendered me unfit to adjust back into the culture I originally came from because I had assumed that the otherwise progressive society that I believed North India to be (especially Chandigarh and New Delhi) was also professionally progressive. This was unfortunately not the case as I observed. In my experience women in southwest India fail to an extent to receive equal respect socially, be it a wedding ceremony where they are seated separately or another celebration where they eat after the men or even within the limits of their home, however, they are not subjected to professional sexism *as much*.

The urban northern region I grew up in has a culture where women are not respected in the professional environment despite the fact that I could see, since the time of my parents and grandparents, nearly as many women working at equal or higher positions as men. In my experience, there have been women in directorial positions in government offices or senior executive positions in private sectors nearly as much as men around me. I am sure they were statistically much lesser in number, but a woman in power was definitely not an uncommon sight. In this same region women own cars, drive to work, sit with men equally to eat and drink, and the working woman is a norm. Women wear the clothes of their choice, joke around and laugh with everyone at a party, and are treated equally in most social circles (on the face of it), *but not at work*.

In this other world (the southwest), where I moved to after getting married, more women were highly educated and enjoyed segregated recreation. It was here that men and women said they were more equal (to each other). I would think that women *were* more equal, my associates or clients at work seldom made me feel otherwise. But, on a whole different level, my social encounters failed to convince me of this.

How was it equal when a huge number of women were not allowed to work yet believed that this was their own choice? How was it equal when none of these women drove the same sized vehicle as their husbands or fathers and believed it was because they could only handle a small car? How was it equal when they believed I was uncultured for going and sitting with men in the family, in my own living room, trying to be the host instead of doing the expected by hiding in the dining room or kitchen with the other women discussing recipes? How was it equal when I was told to wear a bindi every single day (apparently the symbol of a married woman) and wear the mangalsutra forever or 'my husband's life could be at risk'. I was told that it was blasphemy, in our country and our religion, to be married and seen without these two 'lifesaving' accessories. I was asked, 'Do you know what people think of such women (that don't wear these accessories)?' to which I replied, 'I will ask my mother what people thought of her (because she never wore these).'

'Watch how you laugh. Girls don't laugh out loud like boys.'

'You don't sit right. Girls don't sit with their arm on a sofa arm rest.'

'Girls don't drive on the highway.'

'Girls don't talk to men in the family.'

'Girls don't and don't and don't...' and a hundred other things.

I always marvelled how these women, with such an outlandish list of rules to follow, still managed to keep track of the bindi on their forehead throughout the day. Mine would barely stay an hour in one place.

Thankfully, while we were still together, my husband was never ambushed despite my dislike for and rejection of this forced fashion. However, I often wonder, now that I am no longer married, if the learned women there are telling new brides, 'If only she had followed that small little list of don'ts, she would still be married. She brought bad omens! Learn your lesson—don't be like her.'

In particular, one single mother (mother-in-law to a childhood friend) who was a senior executive at a multinational corporation and raised an intelligent, humble son, stands out in my mind. Once, on a visit home, she was complaining about my friend (a highly qualified working professional) and I, 'Both of you, rich girls with no culture and values and with fathers who have spoilt you, will learn your lessons one day.' My friend would not submit to her patriarchal way of life and that is what triggered her to make that remark, I believe. All that I thought of in that moment was, 'How wonderful it would have been if our dads were rich and we were spoiled.' In response, however, I smiled and said, 'That's not true, but would you like another cup of tea with those cashews?'

I am not sure what is more screwed up, a sexist man or a sexist woman. What puzzles me is that societies can give women equal respect in one thing and take it away from them in another. Are these societies actually practising equality, or are these societies Machiavellian, cunningly helping men get what they want from a woman, while duplicitously convincing her to believe it is mutual?

Patriarchy has sowed internalized sexism so deeply among women of all backgrounds and social strata, that it is impossible for only one gender to fight against it and gain any ground. We know that just employment and education do not liberate women from male domination, and this phenomenon of male domination is prevalent throughout the globe. bell hooks said a few decades ago, 'There are many high-paid professional women, many rich women, who remain in relationships with men where male domination is the norm.' This situation hasn't changed much in the ensuing years. Even today, women acquiesce to be in relationships where they are constantly subjected to sexism, where they bury themselves under normalized patriarchy, and inadvertently inherit internalized sexism.

A few years ago, I ran a restaurant in one of the most beautiful places I've had a chance to live: Goa. The enchanting natural beauty of those breathtaking villages with meandering forested roads, some that run through paddy fields, rivers, and springs, together with the Goan warm-heartedness and affability can make you feel like a part of a schmaltzy ballad at all times. Once you start living there, besides all the bewitching rapture that is a revelation, Goa appears to be a twisted, modern part of Indian society indulging in an image of unbridled libertines. It gained independence from Portuguese colonizers (who had been there for four hundred years) much later than the rest of India. I wonder if the prevalent 'twist' in Goa is the effect the Portuguese left behind, because after four hundred years (twice the time the British ruled the rest of India), there are cultural artefacts or public infrastructure that the colonizers developed for the colony, making me believe that the societal norms of the place could also to be credited to them broadly. Seldom do Indians espouse the perspective that, perhaps, we were better off when colonized by the British than another: 'It could have been worse, we could have had no roads,' or 'We could have not known if we were now Indians or still Portuguese!'

The society is majorly matriarchal as I see it. Women run restaurants, supermarkets, fish and meat markets, banks, pharmacies, hotels, and places of worship. They even run liquor stores (uncommon elsewhere in the country due to the stigma attached to women and liquor together). Coincidentally, at the time I lived there (2016–18), the heads of police and the revenue department too were women, in addition to the town councillor of their capital city. Apart from this, all other jobs that we see women doing conventionally in other places in India, like doctors and teachers, are also, inevitably, seen undertaken by women in much greater proportion than men. Most men keep themselves busy managing ancestral property or Rent-a-Bike, Rent-a-Car, and Rent-a-Boat businesses!

In such a society, where matriarchy is the way of daily life, women are still subjugated and voluntarily so in most cases. Women bring everything to the table, whereas the majority of men are unusually indolent and addicted to a life of pleasure: soro-ing* (drinking) away life each day, with no regrets, only hangovers. I sometimes think that if the head of state were a woman, it would do Goa wonders because that is the only seat not held by a woman—yet. Regardless of this, women let the men repress them, deriving some kind of masochistic pleasure out of this arrangement. I say they are repressed and not oppressed because their situation is volitional. Oddly enough, the women here prefer this arrangement for themselves. I credit it to all the inexplicable grey areas that people choose, to justify their life of misery. One such couple I knew during my time there comes to mind.

Theirs was a typical arrangement—a proud and pretty working wife (a graduate in science, teaching in a reputed college) and three adorable children being raised together with her beloved husband. The husband—a generic male chauvinist, megalomaniac narcissist, who primarily eats, drinks, and makes merry—loves and leaves his wife and children at home every night, tucked in warm and cosy for a good night's sleep, to

---

*Soro means alcohol in Konkani.

fulfil his fornicating duties and spend any leftover time with friends. The wife cynically goes around town making surprise checks, searching for the husband every few weeks. But then she chooses to believe each lie that he spins her way. This behaviour is commonplace here. Maybe women believe in lies, despite knowing that they are lies, out of fear of losing the social status they have built for themselves or maybe because believing in lies is more comfortable and convenient than stomaching the consequences of the truth. We tend to deny the existence of anything that is hurtful and requires change or painful growth. Denial is convenient. It is easier than acceptance and ensures dubious comfort. Denial feels right for self-preservation, but is it really self-preservation?

She, like many women around her, has either chosen to stay in denial in the limbo of a no-growth comfort zone to protect herself from agony, or to turn a blind eye to her husband's behaviour because the pseudo status quo of being happily married serves the woman's and the family's economic and emotional needs, however falsely. There are some wives who have accepted that men are like teenagers, habitually astray. So they naturally opt to smack them, kick them, or do whatever it takes to discipline them and get them back home. For some women, the harshest punishment for infidelity, each time it is exposed, is to demand a fancy trip to a foreign land. And then, life is good again.

I cannot decide if the wives beating up their disloyal husbands is a fair reaction to their behaviour, or is this too, domestic violence, an attempt to establish dominance in the relationship? Is it a defence mechanism to compensate for damaged self-esteem, or is it acceptance of the truth, sealed with a customary act of punishment? Is it this spiritless retaliation that convinces a woman that she has resolved the problem? I am not sure what need this retaliation fulfils for these women. They are beautiful and strong, capable of running a house and holding down a respectable job, they manage children and life by themselves but still foster all this fear and low self-esteem, letting emotional dependency override reason.

Women like these, justify a life of disrespect because it is disguised and justify their husbands' betrayal because they believe they will be seen as poor judges of character if they stand up to it. Couples such as them justify patriarchy because it makes them look complete in the eyes of society. This young pair of husband and wife is raising a boy. Two actually. Yet again, I shudder to think.

This particular unethically non-monogamous man (an ace example of part of that community) would often tell me he loved and respected his wife, but he genuinely wished to be in love with more women and that was what caused his infidelity.

I asked him once, 'Your reasons for adultery sound noble, but how would you like it if your wife loved another man while she was your wife?'

To which he promptly replied, 'You are insane! I would kill them both! It is different for women. She wouldn't do it. Why would she do it? She loves me!'

It is different for women. Sure, it is. Isn't that what we have been talking about this entire time?

These same practitioners of disguised feminism (and people in general over my lifetime) have told me many times that I have a beautiful smile; therefore, I should smile less, or men will get the wrong idea. I've been told I should abstain from laughing when men crack jokes, or they might think I am *easy*. If a man made me uncomfortable, I was told, 'You must have sat too close to them,' or 'You are imagining things.' If a man made an indirect pass at me I was asked, 'Oh! What did you say to encourage that?' or told, 'You should have known better than to let it reach that point,' or 'Why did you wear heels to work, who's attention are you seeking?'

After some thirty years of this treatment, a close friend MM said in response to my report of an assault, 'If you slapped him, he must have done something unacceptable.' I was shocked. I was expecting, 'Are you out of your mind? What do you think you were doing?' I did not know this perspective could also be an accepted logic. Especially for a narcissistic (though remarkable) young man, who also has a lot of ill-explained shortcomings and weaknesses—character assassination of women not being one of them.

It sounds peculiar, but that event has stayed tattooed on my mind. I remember it was after dinner and I was with a group of friends at a place that had a detached restroom a long walk away. A drunk six-foot over-confident man parked himself in front of me on my way out of the restroom. He wouldn't let me go, insisting I tell him my name. He slurred his words, 'I know you are alone here. I am doing you a favour by offering company.' At first, I was polite and kept trying to decline his inappropriate verbal gestures. But in the next few seconds, I lost my nerve when he tried to push me into a corner. As a reflex, I slapped him and ran towards my friends. He was disgustingly sweaty, and at the table, I spontaneously wiped my hand on MM's back, apologetically explaining to him that the guy I *had to slap* ten seconds ago was horribly sweaty. Even before I could finish my sentence, I realized what a mistake I was making, I should not have revealed my actions out loud. I was worried that he would tell me *I* was at fault and that my head was not in the right place or ask why I even ventured out alone, but instead he said, 'Point him out to me, which one is he in that crowd?' I did so, and before I could blink again, he strode over and slapped across that man's face three times!

I remember it so clearly that it plays in my head in slow motion. Everything beyond that point is a blur in my mind, given my state of shock and my selective short-term memory. Did my friend overdo it? Perhaps yes. Was his reaction a display of inflated male ego? Maybe. Did he need to show off his machismo to protect a woman who had already protected herself? Probably not. Would we have the same questions if he was a female friend backing up her girlfriend? Definitely not!

Is it possible, perhaps only for a moment, to see MM not as a man but as a *person* who was intolerant of the man who assaulted his friend? To see him as a friend who wanted to have another friend's back? To accept that he was a person who did not tell me it was *my* fault, did not ask any suggestive questions, trusted *my* actions, and for a good sixty seconds of my life, eliminated the sexist bias I was so used to? I don't know why I was seeking validation. Apparently, I needed desperately to be told, just once, that it isn't *my* fault when a man behaves inappropriately, that it isn't always a consequence of *my* actions that he did so, or that I did not *overreact* when I defended myself. And man, those sixty seconds that day sure felt great! Thanks to him.

Not seeing the good in men, blaming flashy machismo for most of their behaviour is like not seeing the good in women, blaming their hormones for their justified reactions. Reciprocal sexism. That's what that is.

If men stop blaming women's hormones and their DNA in general, for every time they hold their ground for something, will that help women become more tolerant and accepting of men and their genuine shortcomings? I wonder. And in reciprocation, will that save men from pretending to be stone-like and emotionless when they are actually crying inside? Will that help men and women, in many cases overloaded with comparisons at work or home, communicate at a more human level, rather than be victims of gender-driven miscommunication? If it is true that all these things will come to pass when men stop blaming women's hormones when they resist men's patriarchal ways, then it would be reasonable to say:

> If misogyny leads to misandry,
> and if misandry is *directly proportional* to misogyny,
> then a *reduction* in misogyny leads to a *reduction* in misandry.
> Therefore, men need to make the first move towards change.

Hence proven!

Unsolicited Suggestion #5

Dear men and women, all these underhanded versions of feminism are worse than outright patriarchy and in-your-face male chauvinism. This is as much a problem with women as it is with men. Just because one society has a higher literacy rate or another one has a higher ratio of working women doesn't necessarily define them as gender-equal societies. It is of greater concern when a society celebrates certain liberations as *privileges* and, in return, expects more from women in the form of gratitude. Women in this milieu believe that they, indeed, are more fortunate than others and thus are indebted to the men around them.

How messed up is this? It is like physical abuse versus emotional abuse. Physical abuse can be seen, it's evident, and leaves a mark. It is easier for the victim, whether or not they can get themselves out of the situation, to decipher that they are being abused—they at least know they need to or wish to stop it. Whereas emotional abuse is not seen, there is no evidence, no physical marks, no clear way to decipher it. This leaves the victim in self-doubt, often believing that they are imagining it all or that it is not that bad, that it is probably their own fault due to their lack of understanding. Victims may think, 'At least I don't get beaten up or cussed at.' The victim of emotional abuse doesn't even know they are being abused; there often isn't even a desire or struggle to get out of the situation or make it stop until it's too late. What is worse?

Dearest men, don't judge a woman or her character by her choice of timing to apply makeup or to be in her pyjamas. Don't tell her how to dress up or what she should or shouldn't wear. Don't tell her it is her fault if she is objectified. And don't tell her it's she who needs to change, it's she who needs to learn, it's she who needs to watch out, it's she who needs to struggle, it's she who should be thankful for a life, it's she who causes problems for herself, because it isn't usually *her*. It's mostly you. In addition, I wish women would pick self-esteem over false social status and not let patriarchy get the better of them for fear of losing what they really do not have in the first place.

It is common knowledge that, on a regular basis (transiting from work to home, in public places, in parking lots, at parties, in the workplace), women deal with all sorts of assaults ranging from catcalling and sexualized slurs to being leered at or being masturbated to or groped, touched, or stared at inappropriately, and many other verbal or physical or sexual threats. For most of these acts, there is hardly a way to prove that it happened and rarely any consequence for the offender, however intimidating and damaging they may be to the victim. Women don't imagine these assaults and they definitely don't enjoy them, so do not tell them, 'Well, I go to those same places, I have never seen that happen.' You are a man; be grateful you haven't had to see it or experience it. *Yet.* Do not tell a woman, 'Oh, come on. I am sure it wasn't that bad,' or 'Are you sure it wasn't by mistake?' Why? Do *you* do that to women by mistake? Don't tell a woman to ignore the assaults or to get over them. When one gender, across all continents, is telling the same story, there is truth to that story. Believe women. Even if you can't feel for them.

It is also common knowledge that if a woman reacts to any such violation, these behaviours or situations can easily escalate, and she will often be the one blamed for the consequences. So, let's teach our sons to neither be prejudiced against other genders nor be dismissive of their gender-specific experiences.

There is, however, one thing that you *shouldn't* do 'because you are a boy' or 'because real men don't behave like that.' You should not dismiss, mock, or snub a woman for saying out loud that something or someone made her uncomfortable. Teach your sons that it is not OK to laugh at sexist remarks or to laugh when other boys or men are laughing at the expense of a woman they know (or don't know) because that behaviour is *not* funny. Tell them not to believe or say things like, 'Oh! Take it easy. It's all in good humour,' because it is not. Tell your sons that when they are in a group of friends and they do not call out one of them for a display of sleazy, disparaging, inappropriate, or abhorrent behaviour towards women, they are equally as regressive and shameful as that behaviour.

We need to tell our sons as much as we tell our daughters that things like assault by a man (who was not raised well) may happen to women, and when it does happen, it is not the woman's fault *ever* and don't ever tell her or make her believe that it is. Tell your sons, that women are neither the property of men nor a trophy or object of desire. Any behaviour implying these things is not alright, so when they do not stand up to those assumptions it is also not alright. Tell your boys that girls must be treated the same way that *they* want to be treated by girls or by anyone else. In the name of love and respect (or just because), don't expect from them or propose any action that you would not want to do yourself. You will not be doing women a favour when you treat them with fairness or behave right and just. You will only be helping yourself become a better human.

One thing my father never said to my mother was, 'I am doing this for you.' He may say this now (he is still the typical man on most days!) but he never said this to my mother when we were growing up. He was never doing things for her nor was she doing things for him. They were both doing things for themselves and for the three children they were certainly responsible for. They were doing things for their family, for their team.

When we start making equality sound like we are doing

women a favour, right in that moment, the game changes to one of inequality. No one is done a favour by being allowed to live a life the way they want to live it. And certainly no one is indebted to anyone else for being allowed to live freely. If we remove this eccentric *allowing* school of thought from our daily lives—again starting from home and starting small—we will be creating an equal society with minimal effort.

An old saying that goes, 'Man proposes, God disposes'. Ever wondered why? Probably, God is a woman is why. She keeps disposing of men's half-baked biased proposals. Maybe it's time we try a different strategy. Let women make the proposals from now on and see if God—see if Nature—disposes of them as readily!

CHAPTER 6

MOM

MOTHERS ARE A PILLAR OF strength for their children, they are the first indications of the sovereignty of God in our lives. *Mother* is not simply a word but a whole universe in itself.

Huh? I did not understand nor relate to any of this until I was twenty-four—a late bloomer. A resolute and unswerving professor at work and a taskmaster at home—for me, that is the only description that fit my mother in my childhood years. I saw her as a highly intellectual professor (well-dressed for work in beautiful saris) and an austere disciplinarian often let down by the middle child (that would be me). Otherwise, she was mostly smiling. She was (and still is) a soft spoken, independent woman of few words who knew what she wanted for herself and how to get the three of us to put our weight behind acquiring what we wanted for ourselves.

Unlike my father, she was always a more conscious feminist in her actions, which mostly fell in agreement with her words. You would think a family run by an independent working woman would share all her characteristics and qualities, that their expressions would be heard and seen as a regular campaign in the house, but that was not the case. She was a silent preacher. In fact, she even conformed to gender roles and made us conform as well. Of course, in the way *she* understood gender roles. And thank God for that, for it did not include patriarchal manifestos such as, 'Girls should cook, boys should play, girls should look pretty, and boys can stray, girls can't laugh or sit a certain way, boys will be boys so let them be that way.'

While we were growing up, she would tell us stories of how she had to struggle to become what she was and how important it is to set a goal for yourself early in life, one that you should never lose sight of. Your goal could be short term, but just having one is the important thing. She would tell us how important it is for every individual to have a job and to earn their own money. It is equally important to take care of your family and always be there for them. She told the three of us that 'it is important to have an occupation that also gives you time for yourself'.

She lived in a very different world and time, growing up. She came from an affluent family that lost everything one day because of a notorious, deceitful uncle, which forced them to move to a new city and start from scratch. Thereafter, her parents only had enough to feed the family. But she worked hard and strove to get herself the education necessary to secure the life of a respectable professor. In her time it was considered indecent for a girl to get a college degree because it meant she would not find a groom, for what man would want to marry a girl as educated as him. However, as if she was ensuring her celibacy, she did not just graduate from college but went ahead and completed two master's programs, one in Hindi and the other in Sanskrit, and completed a Master of Philosophy in Sanskrit. She was always a very bright student, winning gold medals for excellence in college and university (I wish she had passed on those genes to me). She would use all her reward money from academics to help her father set up his own small business, which eventually prospered with the sons helping him take care of it later. Yes, those were different times when small monetary rewards were enough for a conventional start-up if planned well!

She takes pride in calling herself an angel investor for Gupta Vastu Bhandar, the grocery store that eventually became a well-known supermarket in my mother's home town. Her younger brothers own it and have been running it with the same name for the past fifty years.

Having been born in a wealthy family, seen a rich life vanish in thin air without warning, and having worked night and day to make ends meet, she feared for us (my wannabe gangster ambitions would make any parent fearful); thus, she constantly motivated us to have a goal, a dream, and to work towards it. She did redirect all our dreams into practical, dull-but-safe career paths, but to give credit where it's due, she never said a dream was too big.

Like when I repeatedly told her, 'I don't want to learn biology. I want to fly, become a pilot—a fighter pilot and fight for my country.'

To which she would reply, 'I feel it's too early to drop subjects at eleven and think about fighting. Why don't you start by finishing your physics homework tonight, fighter pilots need to be good at that too, and see how things fall in place from there onwards?'

Ha! Indian parents and their obsession with sciences and predetermined career choices. My parents were no different than the millions of others around the country, which shows that it really doesn't take much for a family to turn out to be an egalitarian, feminist family while selectively practising and abiding by the conventions of the society they live in.

While this entire narrative is about a father who unknowingly practised feminism, it would be unfair to not talk about the woman who is equally responsible for raising a son who respects every gender equally. Her son cooks and cleans for his wife and daughter whenever the domestic workers decide to leave them to their wits; works from home to look after his few-months-old daughter while his wife attends to her office duties that, at times, mean working from another country; and loves hanging out with all the girls in the family who have raised him until he was independent enough to now raise girls as a responsible member of the family.

He was always happiest with girls around him—the way some boys are happiest in the company of other boys. Plain and simple. Only, when he was in his awkward teenage phase, his all-boys school left him typically boyish and confused, spending all his time with his schoolmates playing cricket and video games. Nonetheless, having been surrounded by an independent, working mother, two strong-willed older sisters who always had his back, and a childhood friend (a girl) who helped him with homework since the age of three (until he eventually learned to do it himself), he figured out early on that women were an absolute necessity for survival and mostly smarter than the men around. He really did! My mother played a huge role in him having such epiphanies. She never treated him differently, unlike my father, who scolded the son more than the daughters, fearing that Indian boys tend to become smug, and he did not want such a son in his house.

I have never been able to tell who the king of our castle was. In most families it's either/or, but in ours it was both parents. Sure, it could be said that hierarchy is important to maintain discipline, but we are talking about a home, and the only proper hierarchy there should be is, parents above children. In our house, finance was always my mother's area of expertise. Back in the day, the atypical professor of Sanskrit loved banking and taxation and even today cannot give up her Bloomberg TV time. My father was the master planner of everything, but he based his plans on financial feedback from her. Obviously, he would never have admitted to it then. Now after forty years, he has come around to openly accept that, for our household, she was always a better financial and accounts manager than him. Never too late!

The two of them fight like most parents do (I *hope* others fight this much), but they never fought in front of us very consciously. What I mean is we never heard our father say in front of us that our mother didn't know something, nor would she override his word and tell us secretly that it was okay if we didn't want to do what he told us to. They both supported each other's decisions—at least in front of us—so we respected and abided by them too. We could never escape any punishment because if we took our case to my mother, she would just tell us, 'All I can do for you is tell your father that you came to me with it.' Damn! I wasn't joking earlier. We were literally living in an army training camp. Well, it's very different now that they are older and have evidently and mutually developed much less tolerance.

But growing up it was very different. They supported each other's decisions and they both made rules for us. They were equally strict, but they made us have fun too when we'd been good for a while. They taught us to be respectful and kind and to be humble to everyone irrespective of their position and education (unless someone meant to harm us).

It might be said that this arrangement really is not any different from most households. But then again, most of *those* households are not the ones wrestling with multiple issues of inequity, and those are not the ones who are seen struggling every day. Trust me when I say that there is more inequality than meets the eye.

Nirmal Gupta, my mother, the Sanskrit and Hindi scholar, also taught us to reason with and question everything that we read and saw. So much so, that we started questioning the two of them! I am sure she didn't anticipate that. Religion is not a sensitive topic in my house. In fact, my very religious parents also let us question religion and God. Mother told us, 'Don't just believe it because you are told to or because it is written in a book.' She said it is good to have faith but it is also important to have doubts. This quote from Ali Sina, an Iranian-born Canadian activist, resonates with what my mother taught us about faith and doubt, about questioning before believing:

> Doubt is the greatest gift we can give to each other. It is the gift of enlightenment. Doubt will set us free, advance knowledge, and unravel the mysteries of this universe, but faith will keep us ignorant.
>
> One of the hurdles we have to overcome is the hurdle of tradition and false values imposed on us by thousands of years of upbringing. The world still values faith and considers doubt evil.... The word *faith* means belief without evidence; *gullibility* also means belief without evidence. There is no glory in faithfulness. Faithfulness means gullibility, credulity, susceptibility, easy to fleece. How can one be proud of such qualities?
>
> *Doubt*, on the other hand, means the reverse of the above. It means being capable of thinking independently, being capable of questioning and being skeptical. We owe our science and our modern civilization to men and women who doubted, not to those who believed.

My mother would take events from the epics of Mahabharata and Ramayana and ask us to look for the real meaning within the stories. She would quiz us to test our cognitive analytical behaviour (or so I like to believe) by throwing questions at us:

- What did it mean when Sri Hanuman brought an entire mountain of medicinal herbs for Lakshman?
- Did Sri Krishna literally lift an entire mountain on his pinky finger to save the villagers from the rainstorm?
- What do they mean when they say Ravana had ten heads?
- Do you think Gandhari literally blindfolded herself to give her blind husband company, or did that mean something else?

Her objective wasn't to challenge the great epics but to encourage us to think for ourselves, to look for metaphors in stories, to understand the bigger picture when reading history, and perhaps to channel our energy into reading more than quarrelling with each other the entire time. I am not sure how well these lessons in reasoning worked out for her and my father because I got a little ahead of the game and ended up liking Ravana more than the other characters in that epic and more than my father could accept. Thanks to cognitive development in my formative years, I think Ravana is pretty cool!

My father never participated in such 'wasteful' activities (though he did not object to them) and preferred for us to assist him in opening the car hood and checking the engine or in examining the main distribution board. Our role was mostly the torchbearer, where we were expected to shine the light at an angle that was never satisfactory for him. Neither did he object to her ostensible methods of 'estranging' his children from the faith of God, in whom he believed and to whom he prayed every morning without fail.

The three offspring of such a set of parents turned out to respect—and respect equally—their religion and those of others, while also taking pride in being born into their own because of the freedom of thought, the freedom of method of practise, and the knowledge of the all-inclusive nature of religion that our parents taught. Whether we believe in the conventional idea of religion or not, whether we believe there is a God or speak of Nature, whether we practise one form or the other or none is immaterial as long as we respect ourselves and all human beings. This is what my mother would tell us.

I talk about religion here because I see patriarchy as a form of religion. I believe it was adopted as a uniform code by people from differing religions and cultures who would otherwise not tolerate each other, but who deep down, were all unified by the same hymn of sexism. The faithful defend this redundancy by using expressions such as 'It is our culture', 'It is a tradition since time immemorial', 'It is written in the scriptures of the *x*, *y*, or *z* book', 'It is the way of our ancestors', 'That is the way of life', and 'Who are we to question?'

We are *everyone* to question whenever conventions no longer make sense. We ought to ask questions when a blindly followed tradition fails to justify itself and fails to respect one human being as much as the other. Questioning is only prohibited in fear when the answers are injurious to the faithful's reputation and privilege.

We fear to question when we fear the reaction of the one being questioned. We avoid asking questions we know the answers to because we also know that there will be no acceptance of those answers by the ones being questioned. We convince ourselves that they are the ones to decide for us. We fear questions because we fear that the knowledge they bring will cause a rebellion among the questioners—we fear that knowledge will cause unrest and imbalance, that it will shift the seat of power.

To grant freedom of choice and expression can do more harm than good: this is a tenet of patriarchy. And that's exactly the mistake, some would say, my mother, consciously, and my father, subconsciously, made. Our freedom of choice and expression made us feminists, yet we are highly respectful of tradition, culture, and religion. No damage done!

Unsolicited Suggestion #6

Dear women, there is no such thing as being overqualified, be it for a job or for becoming a bride. If you are overqualified in a particular environment, then you are in the wrong place and need to find the place and people that are right for you. I know so many women or parents of young girls who fear that, if their daughters are educated beyond a certain limit, they will never get married. That was my grandparents talking in the fifties and sixties, and they were proven wrong! Isn't it time we stop believing and feeding that misconception? Unlike other girls in her town who were making families proud by getting married at twenty-one, a very close American friend of mine was looked down upon by her entire town because she did not bear children by the age of twenty-six. Instead, she chose to take up a PhD course at that age, and to her Texan community, that meant another five years down the drain.

It is also true, in this country, that if a woman is unmarried until a certain age, she is considered a failure or frowned upon and considered suspicious. But if a man is unmarried until a later age, it is believed there is a dearth of suitable girls for him because he is, obviously, a diamond, and another diamond, worthy and fitting, is naturally hard to find. Once found, that lady is never valued like a real diamond anyway, so why does he make an effort to search for her in the first place? In the end, wives (from faceted diamonds to diamonds in the rough) are all made to submit to the wills and wits of domineering men.

Are these men—who suppress women with ambitions and women who are their equals (or better)—really to be blamed for their behaviour or are their parents or society to blame? If only blaming and nitpicking could undo a problem so deeply ingrained in every society! One of the many hapless reasons for the still strong, age-old, multi-layered oppression of women is a blind faith in patriarchy. Every person, every entity, and every society needs a system on which to run, but at the same time, every system requires overhauling time and again. Weeding out the unnecessary growth of regressive ideas is necessary if we want the society to not collapse under the load of inequality that patriarchy fuels.

Dear mothers, stimulate your children's minds to observe and question gender-based biases. Confronting and questioning irrational social dogma, upheld mostly by one dominating gender, will reverse the dumbing down of twenty-first century human relationships it causes. Teach your sons (even more so than your daughters) to question the rationale behind these established patriarchal orthodoxies that place women below men. Teach them to question the rules prescribed by patriarchy for each gender so that as adults they are able to tell right from wrong. Encourage them to question both their parents when they see reason. And perhaps, when they lead by example, our societies will become more humane.

My mother lent me a sloka,* from amongst her favourites, for this chapter:

Where women are honoured, divinity blossoms, there Where women are dishonoured, all actions remain unfruitful, no matter how noble they may be.

It's high time we respected women, considered them equal. Even if for the selfish purpose of reaping the fruits of your actions. Just do it!

---

*Surprisingly, this verse comes from the *Manusmriti*. Verse 3:56, available at www.wisdomlib.org/hinduism/book/manusmriti-with-the-commentary-of-medhatithi/d/doc199834.html.

CHAPTER 7

BUT WE *ARE* EQUAL

There is no doubt that, in these milieux, much progress has been made with regard to gender equality, following feminist activism, cultural shifts, legal reforms (e.g., laws against sex discrimination) and changes in institutional policy. Gains for girls and women in education have been especially impressive. And yet...misogyny is still with us.

—Kate Manne, *Down Girl: The Logic of Misogyny*

MY FATHER HAS A KNACK for embarrassing his children in front of others in ways unique to him. When the three of us were kids, he didn't interact with us or smile much, but he would insist on randomly dropping us off at school or college for an exam. Then right before the start of the examination, he would come into the room with a big, strange smile and wish everyone in the room 'all the best' in a loud and stern voice. I would often wonder if anyone knew he was my father and whether I should be embarrassed by this public display or if they knew that he never wished us 'all the best' at home before an exam. Who was I kidding, they all knew he was my father. Before leaving the room, he would call out my name, then say, 'Beta, don't worry, you will do well,' and make sure they knew he *was* my dad!

On one such random surprise visit to the campus—perhaps because he had the time or maybe he wanted to use the men's room—he decided to take a tour of the entire building. At the time, I was in architecture college and certainly did not want to be the only twenty-year-old in college whose father did rounds of the campus to check if all the facilities were up to the mark. But there is no reasoning with Dr Singla. On this particular day, while he was on campus, he noticed the men's and lady's rooms. Since they were not occupied, he inspected each in turn. He then went straight to the principal's office.

He told the principal's assistant that he was there to discuss something of grave importance with the principal. He explained that he had to rush back to his duty hours at the government hospital, so he would only need a couple of minutes of his time. The assistant led him into the principal's office. After spending a few seconds introducing himself, my father engaged the principal.

'What is the men to women ratio at this college?' Dr Singla asked.

'Very few boys take up architecture,' the principal said. 'This has been a trend for many years. So, there are fewer boys than girls in recent times.'

'Why is it then that you have two men's rooms and only one for the women?'

'This is a fifty-year-old building and that is how it was designed and built, originally,' the principal replied, 'because there were none to maybe a handful of women studying architecture at that time.'

'So there are two men's rooms with two cubicles and six urinals each, making them available for use by sixteen to twenty men at a time,' said Dr Singla, 'and only two to three cubicles in the ladies room—I didn't go further inside to check exact numbers to avoid intrusion of privacy—for an entire institute that has more women than men?'

'Well, we have recently changed one of the men's room to a common room with that same observation in mind.'

Dr Singla complimented the principal, 'That was a good intention, but did you check if this idea is working? The first thing seen inside those toilets is the row of urinals. Do you think women will enter if they see a man standing at the urinal,' he reasoned, 'or by just the thought of seeing one they will avoid using the common restroom? There will still be men using two rooms and women will only be comfortable using the one that is exclusively for them. Unless you build a cubicle to replace the urinals.'

This *was* actually the case. The principal got to thinking and thanked my father for pointing out the situation. Dr Singla left it at that, before he got further delayed for work. When my father retold the conversation later, that was the first time I had heard that the other men's room was actually for common use. None of us knew about that. The next day, I shared the news with my friends, and they too were surprised to learn this after two years of already being at the campus. We decided to start using it then, whenever ours was full, but it remained a very intimidating and unpleasant task with failed efforts. The principal retired from the chair before he could (even if he wanted to) make any restroom changes. My class graduated three years after that and the situation remained the same. It has been fifteen years since graduation, and I haven't been back to the campus yet, but I am hoping, since the institute finally has a woman chair, things might have become more equal for all—at least in the stalls if not in the lecture hall!

Clearly, I get my love of toilets and their design (more of an obsession, really) from my father. However, as an architect, I am guilty of designing my projects with uneven distribution of women to men's bathrooms. I was neither the one spending money to build them nor an authority on public use of such projects, so I had to drop my arguments for appropriate distribution whenever the client would debate that they were, indeed, following government guidelines. After all, it was 'still an equal *size* for both'. They could not understand why I was pushing them to waste precious square feet on extra toilets for women.

I wish I had found Caroline Criado Perez's *Invisible Women* earlier to support and explain my reasons why women should be given more toilet space than men. I would have had to carry a little less guilt on my poor shoulders. Her extensive research highlights lesser-known facts of everyday life:

> 50/50 division of floor space has even been formalized in plumbing codes. However, if a male toilet has both cubicles and urinals, the number of people who can relieve themselves at once is far higher per square foot of floor space in the male bathroom than in the female bathroom. Suddenly equal floor space isn't so equal.
>
> But even if male and female toilets had an equal number of stalls, the issue wouldn't be resolved, because women take up to 2.3 times as long as men to use the toilet. Women make up the majority of the elderly and disabled, two groups that will tend to need more time in the toilet. Women are also more likely to be accompanied by children, as well as disabled and older people. Then there's the 20–25% of women of childbearing age who may be on their period at any one time, and therefore need to change a tampon or a sanitary pad.

Well, in my defence, even if I could have elaborated this well back then, it is improbable that men in my industry, or any other, would understand and make amendments to such discrepancies. I don't suggest this low probability of resolution because men generally have poor logic and reasoning skills (I will not get into these well-known yet controversial facts here) or because they want women's bladders and hygiene to suffer but because they really believe they are being fair and equal in this instance. Just like they are fair and equal when it comes to the lack of toilets in public places and highways, altogether. 'Women can't complain. There aren't even toilets for us men at such places, but we manage.' By managing they mean finding a bush or a wall to relieve themselves. I really wish women could do their business behind bushes or facing a wall—what a blessing that would be!

One of my closest friends is obsessed with toilets and the state of their use in the world. So much so that she spent years researching the condition of public toilets at transportation hubs in Mumbai (Bombay). Later, she even worked, voluntarily, for a considerable amount of time towards the solutions, but in vain. So much for the love of the loo!

Albeit T. Mittal was made fun of for her passion for toilets more than I ever was. I've never understood why it amuses professionals in our field to hear about her desire, since the age of twenty, to improve the state of toilets in our country.

In 2019, I was visiting Mittal in Mumbai, and on my second day there we decided to walk the city and make a trip of it. Mumbai, like most metropolises around the globe, is a city majorly dependent on public transportation and on walking to access work and other places. It had been almost a decade since our adventures together being roommates in New York. In that time, we had not done something of this sort, to venture out on foot. After our college years, we had spent a lot of our lives between home and work in the comfort of cabs or our own air-conditioned cars.

That day, we were reminded of how our cities are so ill-equipped with public facilities and that our bladders were not as efficient as they were in our twenties. After walking and searching for a toilet for a good thirty-eight minutes, I could no longer hold it in. So, we decided to spend a few hundred bucks on getting our eyebrows done at a fancy salon (neither of us really needed the service) just so I could use a clean toilet.

A clean toilet was desperately needed, especially because it was *that time of the month*. Yes, women do venture out on a day-long city tour on foot even on those days and enjoy it. Another myth I busted that day—women are not irritable because of their period; they are irritable because on those days they mostly can't find a decent toilet to do the necessary unless they are home. That being a primary factor why they would rather stay home than venture out during that time. The next time a man judges an irritable woman at work, blaming her hormones for her behaviour, I suggest he do some introspection to rule out first, whether he is the cause of her irritation, or then go take a look at the nearest toilet available to her.

There is a lot of talk (and mostly just talk) about the dearth of toilets in rural areas by government agencies, where women have to go to farms to relieve themselves. However, historically there has been a lack of focus on women's public facilities in urban areas. Policymakers often stress the need for such utilities only in rural areas, considering the hygiene and, more importantly, the safety of women in these locales. However, we forget that the safety of women in urban public areas is also similarly compromised and exposes them to physical health risks due to a phenomenon termed as 'toilet avoidance'.

It is assumed that a toilet in every home in a city satisfies urban planning needs for bathroom facilities for any development. However, this does not take into account that the more urban a population is, the more public utilities it will need. Believing, that because men manage without public facilities so should women, is a totally baseless argument. Men are perfectly fine with relieving themselves in public, regardless that it is a disgusting and a highly inappropriate sight for anyone other than the one relieved and a sanitary nuisance to boot. But women won't and can't pee in public, making it a necessity to have toilets for them at all public access and transport points. No doubt, men will still find satisfaction in for-display peeing; therefore, governments can cut costs by limiting public toilets for men in such places.

Again, from Perez:

> [In] December 2014, Bombay's high court ordered all municipal corporations to provide safe and clean toilets for women near main roads. Ninety-six potential sites were identified and Bombay's local government promised 50 million rupees (around $700,000) to build new toilets. But a year later, reported online women's rights magazine *Broadly*, not a single brick had been laid. The fund allocation lapsed in 2016.

For nearly ten years in India, I have had to travel in overnight buses from one place to another as that was the fastest and most available mode of transport. My most frequent trip was a 450-kilometre journey each way, whether I was travelling southwards from Pune to Goa for work or frequently northwards from Pune to visit my husband's family in his home town. I either had to dehydrate myself for the ten-hour journey or be prepared to get off the bus on the highway (which runs through farms and jungles), manage a spot neither in the pitch-dark bushes nor visible to high-beam highway traffic, finish the task before a stray animal spotted my posterior, and then run for it before insects could trespass the bare bottom. Imagine the blessing if you are on your period on top of it all. How I dreaded these overnight bus rides, making a dozen trips to the toilet at home before boarding, knowing well that it would still not change my fortune for the night.

I observed the same dire situation in richer and, supposedly, more developed countries like the United States, England, and in Europe. Often, unless a cafeteria allows outsiders to use their toilets, there is no restroom for women for miles around in open public places. For these prosperous countries to have only a few more facilities than the less-developed countries (which may have none) cannot really be termed a commendable job on their part. It's just common sense. I have seen girls relieving themselves on the sidewalk in Times Square throughout the New Year's Eve parade, and that is just one example. Obviously, this is not just a bias against women, because toilets are missing for men, women, and all other genders. But I believe it stems from the same patriarchal mindset that thinks, if men don't need it, neither do others.

I have tried to compensate for the lack of appropriate facilities for women in my own small ways, having learned from my father who spoke about it undiplomatically on most occasions, and from Mittal, who took pride in her commitment to the same. This confirmed that we were from two families who, despite having lived in and experienced life in different parts of the country, were still equally passionate for the cause of safe and equitable facilities for women. Therefore, we were not as amusing or unique in our obsession over the need for toilets as we may seem to be.

The office I set up for my architectural practice reserved the bigger and better toilet for female clients and the women of the office and the smaller one for all the men to use, irrespective of their position in the office. They might have thought it an unfair arrangement for men, but they never said anything because they knew it was fair to the women.

My restaurant (my other business) was in the state of Goa, a society run by women and fed by tourism. The restaurant was on one of the most well-known streets, full of night clubs and guest houses, along a section that led to a particularly famous beach. I was grateful to the police station in that area for letting me use their toilets throughout the construction of the restaurant as there were no other toilet facilities, even in such a tourist destination. All night, local women could be seen setting up temporary food stalls and vendor booths to serve the all-night party goers. Despite this activity, there were no facilities for women anywhere. I decided the toilets on the restaurant premises would be for all to use during the hours of operation, and slowly, news of my facilities became known around the neighbourhood. Girls would come throughout the night (we were open all through the night) from other clubs and restaurants because they could not find clean toilets, or toilets at all, at these places where they paid heavily to drink and dance.

My beautiful garden bistro was gaining popularity, not just because of the toilets, but the local authorities (men, of course), intolerant of women coming from another state (i.e. my business partner and I) and running a good business gaining popularity, sent me a notice saying my toilets were illegal. Apparently, my toilets were illegal in a country where the government goes door-to-door giving people money to build toilets accessible to women, even on agricultural lands. I did not know what these authorities hated more, my restaurant doing well, the available-to-all toilets *not* built by the government and still gaining popularity, or women other than their own doing something better than them (the men). Thereafter, my business literally went down the shit-pot. It probably didn't help that I refused to pay those men extortion money after they called my *legal* structure illegal! People come from around the globe to Goa to set up various tourist-oriented businesses. Right after, the local authority for our neighbourhood successfully created unfavourable circumstances for a few too many businesses that were then forced to pack up and leave. Oddly enough they were all run by non-local women. My guess is they couldn't take any more women proving to them that they could do better business.

Nonetheless, be it this particular place and people or any other; if toilets are missing equally for men, or if men have to face extortions as commonly as women, in the end, it's about these being less adverse events for men than for woman—whether it is having to pee in the bushes or having to pay bribes. After all, we all know, between men and women, which one has to really bend over (and squat on weeds) to make those choices.

There is no denying that there has been much undebatable improvement in equality for women. For instance, an entire day dedicated to them (after decades of tireless efforts by women themselves) now celebrated by men. What else can women ask for? Somehow, it seems like Women's Day, celebrated globally on 8 March, has become a bit of a lost cause in the last few years. Like the snooze button on our alarm clocks to which we become desensitized. Of course, there is a positive aspect to this behaviour: we hit the snooze button proactively to allow ourselves to go back into a deeper slumber until it makes noise again. Desensitizing oneself to social issues—like they are repetitive alarms, knowing that they are going to come and go, over and over—is an all-too-common phenomenon.

Similarly, after having fought its way into existence for over a century, Women's Day is recognized in most countries as either a day for protest or the celebration of womanhood.

However, what it really does is help businesses sell more that day in the name of women, while no one knows why it is being celebrated in the first place. Men buy gifts for or wish their mothers, wives, bosses, colleagues, and friends a Happy Women's Day, with undeniable enthusiasm. Although, it seems more like a 'I don't know what it's for but since it says woman and you are one, here's a Happy Day to You,' or a 'Hey woman, there is a day for you. Happy now?' kind of day. The best ones are those on social media with flowers and balloons, thanking all the beautiful women in a man's life, that document the husband cooking and cleaning (inefficiently) for them that day (making sure they take a dozen pictures of their labour), so these women can be recharged for the rest of the 364 days of household work that they do alone.

There is not a doubt in my head that these men indeed feel bad for women having to do all this labour, but they don't know any alternative. They cherish these women in their lives; acknowledge their hardships; respect them; love them for all the love, support, and care they get from them. They openly display all these emotions on 8 March and then hit the snooze button again until next year. I would like to believe they genuinely do not know what to do with and for women the rest of the year. I don't blame men for not knowing that all the hardships of women they are acknowledging that day are in fact inflicted by their own ignorance and narcissism. Women are celebrated that day for emerging victorious from the adversities of patriarchy. A system that these same respectful men (and some women) consider holy, knowingly or not.

Wouldn't it be great if women were acknowledged and treated equally in a real sense, if men equally divided the load of unpaid domestic work and social responsibilities with women for all days of the year and not just one and we instead celebrated

8 March as No Women Day? Imagine, one day in the whole year, for old time's sake, when men can celebrate the spoils of history, where men can get a break from women, can ignore them and think of them as second-class citizens (instead of thinking like that their whole lives)! Men could go out, party, forget women exist, and leave all the responsibilities for women to manage for an *entire day*. A day when men can practise celibacy and a day-long fast to mark this celebration of the absence of women. They will then definitely deserve such a day after bearing only 50 per cent of the daily domestic and social load that women actually bear for the remaining 364 days of a year. Moreover, since most men largely rely on and respond to rewards for any domestic work done, this day would be the least that women could do to reward them after a year-long practice of equality against their natural inclinations. *That* is when women might be able to say, 'We *are* equal' (at least at home).

Unsolicited Suggestion #7

For centuries, women have led the way towards equality for us, for all men and women of the twenty-first century: from the first ever feminists—the English writer Mary Wollstonecraft in the eighteenth century, Emmeline Pankhurst in the nineteenth century, the Americans Elizabeth Cady Stanton and Susan B. Anthony in the same era—to exceptional women like the Polish–French physicist Marie Curie; Sophie Blanchard, who was the first professional female balloonist; author and American aviation pioneer Amelia Earhart; Justice Ruth Bader Ginsberg, the second female justice in America; Oprah Winfrey, the celebrated talk show host, writer, and actor; and Zaha Hadid, who single-handedly reinvented architecture for the world.

There is no dearth of brave and foresightful Indian women who have helped millions of women around the world find their place in a male dominated world and gain basic rights to a respectful life in the society: eighteenth and nineteenth-century social reformers and pioneers in education Savitribai Phule and Pandita Ramabai Sarasvati (an early emancipator of women); the physician Rukhmabai, who filed and fought a case against her own child marriage in 1884–87; Kalpana Chawla, the first Indian woman sent by NASA into space; living legends in the field of sports like P. T. Usha, Babita Phogat, Mary Kom; and all the women leading the way in the Indian Armed Forces and in Indian politics.

These women, known or unknown, famous or living next door, have fought for all women, including today's generation, to be able to enjoy privileges that are often taken for granted now. When it is said that women want transit seating or parking lot reservation quotas, or education and employment quotas, but do not want to work hard for or earn them, or when it is said that women will just end up having children and leaving jobs, these sentiments issue from a place of high ignorance, privilege, or both. Women do not reproduce by themselves, nor do they reproduce as a hobby or to kill time. Although, wouldn't it be wonderful if women started reproducing by themselves, without remotely needing men to intervene or enable the process, having already discovered that they can feed and pleasure themselves much better. It might be fair *then* to blame women for procreation!

What's fascinating is that India has had many brave and dynamic women warriors, leaders, and reformers over the past hundreds of years, all extensively biographed in books. Even from the first through seventeenth centuries, before the Portuguese and the British came and turned our heads around. Sure, the British left Indians more eloquent in a language that helps to rule half the world and established a progressive railway and transportation system in the country, but even more impressive is that they further fuelled the ongoing deterioration of the status of women. Indian men gladly welcomed their patriarchal mindset, so it wouldn't be completely fair to credit the English alone for gender inequality in India. Interestingly, Rukhmabai's infamous child-bride case of 1884–87 raised significant public awareness and debate across several topics, most prominently law versus tradition, social reform versus conservatism, and the reality of feminism in both British-ruled India and England.

Dear men, you may think today, that all of this has nothing to do with you directly, or that you could never have controlled conquerors, governments, or countries that were making gender biased policies at the time, nor can you individually interfere with the policymakers for nations or even local bodies now. You may think that whatever happened in the past is a bygone, that whatever gender bias data gaps are in the planning of our modern world, are now out of the control of any man or woman.

'What can we tell our boys in this context? What can children or individual adults possibly do? This is something the governments and policy makers must deal with,' you may say.

Well for starters, men, tell your sons that, for the last 400 odd years, women have been doing all the heavy lifting for their own advancement. While you lead by example, tell your sons they can help women with small reforms on their side, starting with controlling the urge to pee in public. It is plain vulgar and uncivilized to pee anywhere other than a toilet, so tell your sons to control themselves in the absence of a toilet. That is one way among many to show respect to women. Even if the toilet is a whole ten feet away, be brave and walk up to it. Don't just pee behind a tree and call it free fertilizer. Only if you do that will you and your sons know how difficult it is for women to control their need to pee and how important it is to have more facilities in public places and on highways. Maybe then planners and teams working, even unknowingly, with such gender-biased data for urban and rural planning will be urged to start thinking about and making reforms that will increase equality for all in a practical sense.

Admit to yourself and make your sons understand how dangerous it is for women, in a hundred unfathomable ways, to not have access to such sanitary facilities; how so many places that might seem harmless to you are so unsafe for women; how women get sexually assaulted due to the lack of safe, appropriate sanitary planning for them. This is one of many reasons why women are inherently more scared and guarded than men in public places. Tell your sons women are twice as scared as men in public and rightly so. Even though, you as men may be exposed to potential threats in such unsafe places, they are never the same kind or the same intensity as for women. Tell your sons how it is not something to laugh at when a woman tells them they are scared (even in a crowded place) but that it is something to pay attention to. Just because some women are more fearful and others choose not to admit it, it doesn't mean they are weaker than men. It just means men have been intimidating women long enough, and continue to do so, for them to be eternally frightened and set on edge.

Teach your sons to be the kind of men who do no harm to women, who make sure other men and empty places are something that women don't have to fear. Women are more afraid of infectious disease, sexual assault, or rape than of murder. Tell them, and do understand yourself, that men cannot judge women's fear when they don't qualify for the same terror. Just because a national building code or a building by-law book says a structure or location is a safe and fair design because it is safe and fair for men, does not necessarily mean it is safe and appropriate for women.

It is high time governments used all the gender-based data and research available to assess and reassess the standard laws and rules of civic planning for any habitable area, irrespective of scale, across all countries. We need to tell our boys about the inequitable privileges they enjoy and that they will continue to perpetuate them until someone decides to take up gender inequality as a cause for global reform. The world is not completely oblivious of gender inequality nor totally lacking in intention to change the situation but maybe focusing on the bigger and more prominent gaps that the genders face (for instance, in terms of employment or legal rights), has taken away all the attention from inequalities on the civic-planning scale. Maybe we need more women making such planning decisions at all levels, or we need to educate men to listen to a woman on a team when she says a solution might only work for half the population.

There are obvious social problems in our lives. But for these issues to register in the human brain, they need to be communicated in words loud and clear. Don't assume that just because someone is aware of an issue that they understand it too. Make a conscious effort to tell young boys about the problems that girls face because of such planning gaps all around us, so they become more accepting of these seemingly smaller issues that are actually large issues for the other gender.

Maybe a husband won't gasp in disapproval so loudly if he understands why his wife makes him stop for a toilet break more than twice on a road trip. At times like this, out on a highway, he should be grateful he was not born with a woman's blessed reproductive anatomy, which becomes a health hazard if not appropriately cared for. Women around the world are choosing dehydration to avoid the dangers of roadside jungles, prospective rape sites, out of the way urban spaces, or the dirty looks they might get from their co-traveller in their times of need. That being their set of options is *definitely* something to think about.

CHAPTER 8

BOSS LADY

*We still think of a powerful man as a born leader and a
powerful woman as an anomaly.*

—Margaret Atwood

GROWING UP, EVERYONE IN THE neighbourhood was afraid of
my father because he smiled the least and scolded the most. I
do not remember him ever shouting and scolding—his voice
is loud enough to shatter glass doors (and ceilings)—but his
favourite thing to do was to 'Call them all here', and 'Let them
explain themselves to me'. Mostly, all of us children would take
our disputes related to being cussed at to him because we knew
he was intolerant of this behaviour. Coincidentally, it would
always be one of the boys who used a bad word, and my father
would ask the same question each time.

'Would you like it if the same word came out of *her* mouth?'

In one particular instance, one of the boys said, 'But she
is a girl, girls can't say this.'

'Girls can say everything that boys can,' my father said, 'but
if you would not like to hear it from them, then remember,
they don't like boys who speak like that either. A wrong is a
wrong for everyone the same.'

My parents' motto was the age-old *spare the rod and spoil
the child*. They both believed that discipline is the key to good

child-rearing and that it has to be the same for everyone. Those were the times when smacking children to discipline them wasn't such a thing of horror nor was understood to be the abuse that it is. My father never had to resort to violence though, especially with my sister and me. He wasn't necessarily the same with my brother. He believed, and still does, that 'Boys need to be taught they are not special.' He would say boys are responsible for their actions and should know that there are consequences. He tells my brother, now that he himself has become a grandfather, that he was always harsh with him because he did not want him to think that he could do certain things *just* because he was a boy or that he doesn't *need* to do something just because he was a boy. He gives himself credit for raising a son who adores his wife and daughter not just by showing love with words and gifts or by cooking for them but also by being the night-shift parent for his toddler and letting his wife breathe.

Discipline comes in many forms, but it is only for the good as long as it does not start to make the disciplined hate the one disciplining. That is domination. Discipline is different from domination, and where there is domination there is no love—be it in any relationship. My father did not dominate us, even though that is what his discipline bordered on at times. However, we did look forward to the day of the week when he had night shifts at the hospital, and the three of us could laugh and get all loud and messy for just one day every week. It was like our weekly furlough.

He was a disciplinarian, but he also encouraged us to speak our minds. He would tell us to be brave and to not be pushovers, maybe because he observed that he could push us over so easily then. He wasn't always happy with the little to no fight that we would put up against his discipline. It's a whole different ball game now that he is older. He feels like he is being pushed over by three grown children who bully him into a holiday with them or make him celebrate his birthday and other similar things that he never did for himself in our childhood.

One thing he did like to do (and still does) was talk a lot. He talked to my mother a lot about his work and the politics involved. He loved work gossip, like all men do, but would not admit it. Most men choose to share gossip with their male friends, but some like to come home and discuss work life with their wives. He was the latter. I strongly believe small things like these conversations between my parents made a big difference in my childhood. We grew up thinking that moms and dads come back from work and tell each other all about their respective days, while the kids are passively subjected to work gossip at the dinner table. Surprisingly, I have not seen this rapport between mates very much after I moved away from home. There are men in abundance out there who tell their wives, 'You will not understand. It's work,' or 'Stay out of it,' or the more polite alternatives, 'I am tired,' or 'Why do you want to waste your time knowing.'

These men believe that women can't understand such things. This attitude is just another prejudice people have been conditioning themselves and their children to believe. If men and women keep telling themselves that women will not understand, they will eventually start believing this prejudice without a doubt. Half the time, this prejudice is nurtured by men's fear that by talking to their wives about something they cannot handle or comprehend at work, they might come across as weak and incompetent or lesser than their wife. Some men avoid sharing because they worry that it might be too much information for her. That's where feminism can liberate men. They should be able to express and admit what is hard for them or where they are failing. They need to be told it is all right to not have all the answers. They need to feel equal to all women, not just the ones they are married to and raising children with. Why is it all right for a male friend or a colleague to know your weaknesses and fears but not your wife? Wouldn't telling their wives actually be less embarrassing and more relieving to men instead of telling their male friends and colleagues?

My father never travelled alone even for his medical conferences. He always insisted on bringing my sister to give him company, knowing she was the most diligent student. He felt she could learn something from meeting all the experts in his field of medicine. He would introduce her to all the men and women who had made their mark in medicine in one way or another and tell her to be like them. Seemingly a very small gesture, but in my opinion, it was a very big one—to tell a young girl that she could be like *any* of them. He always told each of us, 'Don't just aspire to be a doctor or some other professional, be the best in that field and aim to lead.'

'Be a boss!' he told us all, especially my sister and me, giving examples of his own female bosses. He admired all those women in power that he came across. He would tell us how the state health secretary, a woman, did a lot of good work. When no one else supported him, she supported his tough decisions as a chief medical officer in the state, despite a lot of political tensions that she had to face as a consequence. He would give us examples of how his female friends from medical college, in the generation before us, had done so well—all the more reason for us to do something bigger, with more available resources. He would make extra efforts to introduce us, as children, to women in leadership positions in medicine, judiciary, revenue, education, or other important careers. He never missed a chance to embarrass us in front of each of them, saying 'See? You have to become like her one day,' or if it was a man he would say, 'See? You have to become his boss one day.' He has always believed it's women who are better suited to be leaders (apart from himself, of course!).

It was quite tortuous to be dragged to these awkward encounters, and we would wish for an escape from him, understanding little what these encounters were actually doing for us as children. Never did it occur to me that those introductions were the reason my siblings and I have no concept of men being better than women as leaders. As a girl, I also believed women were supposed to lead like my father was always telling his daughters, while his son understood he would be lucky to have a woman as his boss when he grew up! Surprisingly, he never said, 'Be like your mother,' who was an academic gold medallist, a language professor, and then a deputy director of education for colleges in the state. Well, that was one of the ways we knew he was a *normal* patriarchal man; he never acknowledged his wife's achievements (phew!). I had to step out into the real world as an adult to discover that it was completely the opposite of what we were brainwashed to see and believe in all those years. People don't like women to lead. No way!

Despite having age-old evidence of successful women leaders and contemporary researchers and experts in the fields of leadership or behavioural psychologies publishing extensively on the subject, we fail to imagine women in leadership as commonly as men. Acceptance of the phenomenon—of a woman in a leadership role—on the ground level is a whole different ball game of friction and resistance. Then again, even if women are more competent and more qualified than an average, overconfident man, they are still rarely given opportunities of the same scale and importance as men. Employers conveniently fall back on the presumption that a woman wouldn't be able to handle the job or simply that men in the boardroom would rather listen to another man than be distracted or intimidated by an intelligent woman making a good point or giving directions.

I have fortunately experienced this first-hand on more than one occasion. During conference call arguments with certain corporate clients (who were not going to win), I have been told to 'put a man on the phone' because they refused to discuss the issue with a woman (me) and apparently since they were a very large company of a certain reputation therefore, the objection 'we cannot discuss financial issues with a woman'. As if all those words together even made any sense. They insisted that I ask my husband to call back instead or if there was another man in office to put him on the call. I could have even put my office boy on call, for all they cared. This when everybody on either side was aware that they were speaking to a woman who ran the firm as an equal partner, the other equal being my husband (mistaken to be my guardian-caretaker-spokesperson-supervisor). This attitude was so prevalent that my husband would get offers for partnerships, telling him it was better to have a man with him since the business involved construction and dealing with government offices. 'She is obviously going to give up soon when it gets harder,' they'd say. At another time, a client refused to pay a contractual fee, and when I called to check what was causing the delay, he stated an obvious reason that I had overlooked, 'It doesn't look good for a lady to call and ask for money,' he complained. 'Tell your husband to call if you want your fee.'

A highly educated senior officer of the Indian Administrative Services once told me, 'Your company profile is amazing, but we cannot commission you because you will not be able to come to the all-male meetings in such government projects.' In other words, the men won't like it. Of course, they gave the commission to someone else, a man much less qualified. No points for guessing that. I had never seen my mother give up a job or any other work because it got harder or heard my dad telling me that all those amazing women I met, only worked until it got harder. So, I did not understand that argument these men were putting up. Nor did I know, before this, that men do not like women in boardrooms or discussing projects with them as an equal stakeholder. To boot, I definitely did not know before any of this, that every time a man starts feeling less competent than a woman, he compensates for that insecurity by *telling* her she is a woman. Like it is a bad thing. And so, she should stop talking.

In his book *Why Do So Many Incompetent Men Become Leaders? (and how to fix it)*, Tomas Chamorro-Premuzic presents reliable evidence that shows women generally outperform men as leaders.

> Most notably, in a review of forty-five studies on leadership and gender, Alice Eagly, a professor at Northwestern University, and her colleagues found that women were more able to drive positive change in their teams and organizations than men were, not least because of women's more effective leadership strategies. Specifically, women elicit more respect and pride from their followers, communicate their vision more effectively, better empower and mentor their subordinates, approach problem solving in a more flexible and creative way, and are fairer and more objective in their evaluation of direct reports. In contrast, male leaders are less likely to connect with their subordinates and to reward them for their actual performance. Men focus less on developing others and more on advancing their own career agenda.

This is coming from a man in the field of business psychology. I am sure some men will believe the contents of this book, if not for research reasons, at least given that it was written by a man (a very learned one at that). I can only hope that Chamorro-Premuzic won't be told his book is biased.

In the decade I spent as a leader, I was able to drive positive change in my organization and got occasional validation for the work I did, like when former employees would return to join the team after spending some time elsewhere. Who doesn't cherish validation for their good work? Surprisingly, it was still a constant struggle to be accepted as a person of authority among bigger clients like the government or other private corporates who, presumably, have been represented by highly educated and well-travelled people; whereas the smaller groups (even clients who were uneducated with farming as their primary occupation) seldom displayed displeasure in such an arrangement, where they had to, more often than not, go by my opinion.

Even in recent times, when I had to sit on the other side of the table, I was reminded constantly by interviewers that I was a woman. This was when I volunteered to turn in my share at the firm and move out during our separation (after years of building and running that beautiful firm) and thereafter decided to go look for work outside. I had men and even women interviewing me, turn around and tell me, 'We know how these husband–wife partnerships work in business' or 'You said your husband was your partner at the firm, so what did *you* do there?'. 'Me? I used to sit there and chew peppermint while I painted my nails all day', I wanted to tell one of them. Some would ask, 'Is there proof that it was you who undertook these responsibilities and not him?' or 'you don't look like someone who could have led such a project'. *Look* like? And this was after I stopped telling them I have run multiple businesses because that certainly wasn't helping. They would definitely appreciate the entrepreneur if it was a man with such a diverse portfolio but for me it meant I was playing around with my husband's hard-earned money while the poor man was slogging himself doing all the work.

Adjectives like bossy, bully, bitchy, arrogant, stubborn, and money-minded are not rare or unheard of for most women with leadership qualities or in leadership roles when they are simply doing their job right. These are in fact the most welcoming and least troubling of possible adjectives or reactions. There have been instances where women have been assaulted or even killed when they show authority over men, who were conditioned to think of them as lesser mortals. We have read about such incidences in the papers more often than not, when a man assaults, rapes, or kills a woman because she dared to shout at him for his misbehaviour. Being scolded by a woman, to these men, is an insult that calls for revenge, obviously. These men will never go ahead and rape a man because the latter scolded or even abused him for not doing his job properly. I do not think any parent could prepare a girl for that kind of dangerous mindset. How can preparation do any good when parents are not preparing their sons to accept women as equals or for situations where a woman could be their boss as much as a man could.

Being called all of those slurs as an adult is one thing but having my professors in undergrad call me similar things was deeply perplexing and deterring, especially since I came from a strangely equal milieu. I remember a confrontation I had with a design professor who graded me poorly without even opening my neatly rolled and taped set of design sheets. He'd called me to his office. It was common there for professors to grade without looking at our assignments and for nobody to care; it was an accepted norm. Most times, however, I could not digest this practice and would reach out to the professors and ask for an explanation of such unfairness.

Customarily, the professors would just dismiss me, but this one asked me to come back again later and see him alone in his office. I was hesitant and a little worried but had to go, so I went. When I reached his office, he pointedly explained that I could not sit and had to keep standing. He then picked up a brand new 2B pencil in a nice ochre colour with a soft pink eraser at the end. The pencil was perfectly sharpened and made me think he was reaching out to draw something. He lifted the pencil and asked me if I recognized what that was.

Thinking I had mastered my fear, and amused at the odd question, I said, 'it's a pencil.'

'No!' he shouted. 'This is you! This pencil you see in my hand is you *and your father*, so you better look at it carefully now.'

The situation instantly ceased to be amusing because I had no idea why he brought my father into this little performance. He definitely did not seem pleased with his own joke, either, so I nonchalantly said, 'Okay.' He then reached out to the pencil with the other hand and before I could take a breath, he broke the pencil in two.

The professor raised his voice, 'And this is how you will break one day!' he shouted. 'This is you in two pieces.'

I was definitely disturbed then, but his huge face purple with rage, the hopeless broken pencil in his hands, and the overly dramatic monologue that extended beyond that act of breaking, were also outrageously entertaining. He then told me to get out of his room, immediately, as if he was worried someone might come in or I might start crying. Neither happened. But to date, I haven't figured out why a fifty-some-year-old man felt the need to tell a twenty-one-year-old girl that she *and her father* would be broken in two. Was it because I did not blindly follow the herd or was it because I'd questioned him, and he blamed my father for that behaviour somehow?

Fourteen years later a friend I had known for just over a year told me something that left me equally bemused. He said, 'I like your father.' However, he had never met him, so I reminded him of that and asked him how could he possibly like someone he hasn't met? I thought maybe he'd had a little too much to drink that evening. He said, 'I haven't met him, but I am sure I will like him when I do.' I wasn't quite following and told him my father wasn't anything like he was probably imagining, and that he better hold his judgment until after he meets him. He quickly added, 'I want to meet the father who raised a daughter like you.' He knew what I was going to say next, that my mother had raised me to be like this, too. So, he immediately continued saying, 'A strong mother will raise a strong daughter, but it is the father who makes a daughter fearless.'

I stutter on the right response to simple compliments like, 'You look good today,' or 'I like your hair,' or 'You have a beautiful smile,' and instantly feel the need to compensate with something like, 'You should have seen me this morning—I looked like garbage!' What that friend had told me was totally unheard of and out of curriculum for me. Hence, I was not practised in my response. How do you respond to something like that? I did not know if that was a compliment to me or to my father or to both of us or was it just a conversation that I should let flow without reacting? How do you respond gracefully to something like that, offhand?

This was the first time it hit me that it actually was my father who raised us all to be fearless yet respectful. And that someone thought *I was fearless*! Besides the genes they give to a child, there are certain qualities and attributes only a father can instil in a child. Fathers are the underrated and unacknowledged teachers of character for a child and these two men knew that (but with opposing appreciation).

This friend was a big, strong, dutiful police officer in charge of the area where I ran my restaurant. He loved to party after a hard day's work, or sometimes days and nights of hard work, in the notorious tourist neighbourhoods known for occasional narcotics use and other abuses. He had seen me physically build a business from scratch—up and running in sixty days. I was mostly riding those painful night buses or driving back and forth, to my husband, home, and architectural practice a good 450 kilometres away every week. My staff at the restaurant and in the office back home was the family I had to equally look after while making sure they also performed the same way in my absence as in my presence. My friend was always appreciative of women and especially women in charge. He was never disrespectful of women or seen mocking or dismissing one, even at his police station. During the time that I knew him, he had two different women bosses in his police department. He would always talk about them in high regard. He felt worse than me when, after two years, I had to shut down this business thanks to the intolerant racketeer authorities in the region and a menacing business partner.

Before I left, he told me, 'All the men in the city said that you would not be able to start a restaurant in this short time, but you did and did it better than them. Then they said, you won't be able to manage it, but you did and again better than them. I have faith in your abilities and intentions and wish there was a way you could keep this business and prove all these men wrong once again.'

This unfeigned appreciation and acknowledgement was momentous to me at a time when I felt defeated. It helped me move forward unencumbered, knowing I did my best according to myself *and* according to those who believed they were better (than a woman) but still could not do it themselves. He has a son of around eight years old and told me that he wishes now to have a daughter, too, so he could raise her to be like me. Praying that it comes true, I feel happy that I have also had the opportunity to cross paths with men who continue to exalt women. He has his flaws aplenty (don't we all) and he definitely isn't a feminist; he just doesn't believe women are lesser than men in anyway nor does he feel threatened or a constant need to be better than them. Another subconscious egalitarian maybe. That men like this will raise a son, leaves me with a sense of relief.

In the same circle as him, there are men who love women as much as he does (they really do—as many as they can at one time) but only as long as these women say yes and play dumb or do not have an opinion or challenge their authority over even the measliest decisions or ideas; men who feel worthy only if a woman asks for help or, even better, if she cries and begs for it; men who like to go boast to other men of how they rescued a woman, who might now be dreaming of being her knight in shining armour (because that's *all* she was waiting for in her life); men with fragile egos and even more fragile self-esteem, who need to put women down in order to feel their own worth; men who get intimidated easily and, thus, mock strong, independent women—women who might have strengths that these men lack in character and ability. They call women names, become vengeful, and look for ways to bring them down, especially if they feel challenged by a woman with a mind of her own. They are grown-up bullies, deriving perverse pleasure by subjecting women to their passive aggressive wrath (and calling it a sense of humour).

There are men like the two chefs at my restaurant, who

could not tolerate working for a team of two women, and so opted to defame, steal, and then abandon their jobs without informing their bosses because they were not answerable to women. And men like my undergrad professors, a homogeneous lot, who wish to see strong women break like a cheap wooden pencil, even if they are harmless humans less than half their age.

Whoever claims that not all men are alike is right. Of course, they are not the same, they are of all different kinds, and it is amazing how these various kinds still manage to inherently practise sexism in unique ways. Then there are the kind of men who have never seen women in business or working independently, married but having their own identity, or those who choose to not bear children in the same timeline as them or not have any at all. One such man, a celebrated, high-ranking officer in the defence services with a beautiful, hardworking, intelligent wife and two teenage children, told me I was gay. He was a client of my architectural firm, who'd been referred by a friend. He presumed I was interested in his over friendly small talk because I was polite (on most occasions) and in one such conversation went on to insist I was gay because, apparently, straight women are not like me. He knew it all! He told me that straight women do not wear black every day or wear corduroy trousers to work more than skirts like I did. This was a prelude to the smutty impropriety that followed.

'Straight women cannot be good bosses like you or manage multiple businesses,' he went on. 'You don't have to hide it from me, I know for sure that you are a lesbian. I have seen enough women like you in my career in the army, and I can help you. Most of them do not know until they try....' He texted this to me that day, uninvited.

Breaking news for Mister Seen-Enough-Women and the likes, who judge women with their earth-shattering insights and knowledge of human beings: women do all of the above! Not all women are the same. They do not have to be homosexual, bisexual, or heterosexual to have leadership qualities, to love wearing only black or white, to prefer pants or skirts, to intimidate weak characters, to run a business and home with the same zeal, to be more educated than men, to want to procreate or not, to have more substance than men—to be self-reliant. When did someone's sexuality decide their abilities and capabilities, or when did their choice of colours and clothes decide which way they swing? In any case, I still wonder how *he* was planning to help me if I preferred women over men? Of course, I forgot, we always need a man to come to our rescue.

Unsolicited Suggestion #8

Sexism and misogyny are not inborn but an institutionalized conditioning of one particular gender since birth, that makes it hard for them to combat prejudice and bigotry against other genders. It is the consistent, dogged encouragement for having been born a boy and the constant comparison of young boys to girls that, ironically, instils insecurities (falsely masked as superiority complex) in them. This results in a lifelong overcompensation for the expectation that boys ought to be better than girls. This expectation is then fulfilled via the suppression and oppression of other genders through violence or mockery. This is not rocket science, just sayin'. It's important for *all genders* to feel equal.

Dear men and women, we should all be feminists. Feminism isn't a tool for females alone, to fight for themselves. It is a tool for men to fight injustice, too. Feminism means life itself is for women as much as for men. If something is wrong for a girl or woman to say or do, it is also wrong for a boy or man to say or do the exact same thing. Wrong for one *is* wrong for the other or it is not wrong at all. Why should you tell your children growing up that it's OK for boys to talk in a certain way but that it is not OK for girls too? No. It is not OK for boys if it is not for girls. Teach them that. Why don't we start telling children '*people* should not do this', or '*people* should not talk like that', or '*people* should not disrespect other people'. Last time I checked, all human beings, irrespective of gender, were collectively known as *people*. Even if just half the men in the grown-up world understood that they were people and that women are people too, there would be far less forced expectation doing the rounds in the professional and domestic worlds of either party. Let's not raise anyone with false beliefs of superiority over others, because let's face it, no one is superior. There is plenty of data to prove that superiority is all in the mind!

Parents, encourage your children to speak their minds. Tell your sons and daughters that anyone can make a mistake and that is all right. Tell them when they see someone doing something wrong, regardless of their gender, to call them out on it. To not keep quiet just because you are a girl, or he is a man. Tell your daughters *and* your sons to command respect, not to demand it. Men, tell your sons that being a man is not reason enough for their wives or their female colleagues and bosses to respect them. Tell them they have to earn respect just like anyone else, but they need to give them a chance when it's their turn and recognize their efforts. Tell them not to respect a man as their superior at work only because he is a man and to not begrudge or resent a woman as their superior because she isn't one. Tell them to give both men and women the same opportunity to prove themselves and set the same benchmarks for them before deciding who deserves respect and who doesn't.

Why is gender equality in workplaces today celebrated as an achievement? The majority of businesses employ women as a token effort and then lay off women first when the seas get rough. Tell your sons about the women at work with you. Talk about them and your male colleagues equally and fairly. Let your sons know from early on that it is normal to have women as colleagues or as superiors. Even if you do not usually talk to your children about these things, you must make an effort. Make an effort so they do not grow up to believe women cannot give orders or run businesses. Make this effort so they do not grow up to become men who are detrimental to a woman's career because she is better at her job than them. Make this effort so your sons do not become the type of men who fall into depression with the thought that they were of less value than a woman. Anyone can be better than them at a given pursuit, and they can be better than anyone at their own—gender has no role to play in it. Make sure they understand that.

My book talks to fathers because I strongly feel fathers are underdogs when it comes to parenting. They could play such an important part in raising their children, if only they would consciously undertake their role as an educator. Daughters do not have to be their princesses, nor do only sons have to be their comrades. They could both be the father's friend or his partner in crime or simply children who need to be taught the right social skills, very consciously, to create a better society in which *they* will be living in the future. Fathers can instil qualities in children that mothers cannot. Fathers can normalize gender equity for sons, mothers alone cannot. Maybe we should give fathers their due recognition and help them take over the role of a caregiver more prominently, thus relieving women of their unending task of constant caregiving. Why should mothers get all the credit for raising a resilient, strong daughter (or for a badly behaved son)?

Why should it be a shock to men when they meet strong, independent women? Why do they believe these women are a rare kind? Let me tell you, wherever *that one* came from, there are hundreds like her. That's what I tell everyone now when they proclaim that they have not met a woman like me before. It's no longer a compliment to me. Sadly, it's an expression of their ignorance and lack of exposure. There are women like me everywhere, and they've been around for centuries before I was born. I am not even half as worthy as the women who have inspired me or those who continue to do so as my friends and acquaintances. These women, in their own homes, are making dozens of sacrifices and compromises each day just to keep men nurtured and content.

I have women friends in my close circle who have experienced things I could not survive if I were in their place. One of them, an entrepreneur, changed her religion to that of her husband and now lives a very restrained life, following those traditions and then defending them every time her parents point out the simple pleasures she is missing in life. Another teaches South Asian history to American graduate students and raises a beautiful stepdaughter, battling her own health issues and all the other daily hazards of being a full-time working mother; one is a government officer (another full-time working mom as are all the others I mention) raising three children all by herself, leaving behind an abusive relationship; there is one who works a job as well as runs a business and is the sole caretaker for the ailing elderly in a family of eight; another comes from a family of all women who have gone through tremendous losses and then come together to help raise each other up to not just feed themselves but to serve their community too; one who is more qualified than her husband (not uncommon) and is sustaining the house and family with her own income while getting constantly condemned, often abandoned, for not doing enough; three who bravely fought their way out of abusive relationships while keeping highly respectable steady jobs; and many, many more women that I have had a chance to know closely. They are all strong women creating their own realities, and in so doing, inspiring other women around them. They don't get rewards for doing any of this nor do they expect one, so the least we can do is acknowledge their efforts and sacrifices because we all know there aren't enough men in this world who can display such strength or sustain through these daily hardships.

Men, let's teach our sons to call these women strong and brave—not difficult! A woman who knows what she wants is a wise one, not a difficult one. She fights her own battles and still stands strong. She is brave, not stubborn or bloody minded. Teach your sons, too, to be inspired by these women and to not resent them for making the choices they've made. Why should only women be inspired by women? Why can't we teach our boys to be inspired by women and to learn from women's experiences? Why can't we teach our boys to never subject another woman to scathing hardships and injustice?

Let's teach our sons to *reject* the irrational dogma of patriarchy, to *reject* the role of a formidable companion who makes a woman stronger by believing what doesn't kill you, makes you stronger. Let's teach our sons to be quality companions instead, who make a woman happier with desirable camaraderie.

Teach your sons to accept *no* from a woman and that that woman could be anyone. Train them to become civilized beings who do not take no as a personal humiliation, who do not seek revenge when that no comes from a girlfriend, wife, boss, or even the lady in the fish market. The onus for change in our sons is upon women as well. Women ought not to fantasize about aggressive, condescending, male chauvinists as partners or contemporaries. There are women who interpret the inflated egos, aggressive displays of machismo, and self-indulgence of some men as virtuous and call it passion or personality. It is a personality but not a good one to say the least. Sadly, some women do derive pleasure in keeping such company, to make up for the insecurities they might possess. It could be to make another woman jealous, or to flaunt feeling better than them, or it may only be because they have been raised to think such behaviour is normal. Inflated egos, macho displays, and self-indulgence are not normal. This behaviour is simply toxic and unhealthy on many levels.

This twisted patriarchal politics, where an aggressive, vengeful, and dismissive man can be an important validation of womanhood, is the cause of our own destruction. This notion tears down the past efforts of women martyred for equality. These chauvinistic men are just momentarily charming; we let them believe in their superiority by encouraging them as fathers, mothers, wives, or girlfriends.

While we are on the subject of superiority, let it be known that there is no superiority complex. There is only overcompensation for some kind of inferiority complex. My very educated sister, who is also a trained psychologist, educated me with this wisdom once, and it has stuck with me for decades now, making more and more sense as I grow older. Such over the top, cocky displays of superiority may seem intimidating but attractive when coming from a man but repulsive and ugly coming from a woman. That is a clue to its unhealthiness. Feminism will emancipate women and men equally by relieving them of the constant pressure of performing and sustaining patriarchy. For men too, it is liberation from the stereotypical images they are forced to maintain.

Men, please tell your sons (and yourself) that when a woman is your boss or performs better in the office it doesn't mean you are worse than a woman or that you couldn't even beat a woman, it just means another person performed better this time. There should be no personal insults associated, just motivation to be like that person. You make your own lives harder by constantly comparing yourselves to women if you imagine them to be inferior.

It's also known that men are weaker than women—it is, trust me. Men have physical strength comparable to but mostly greater than women, but even then, there is not much they have contributed to being so. It is biology. However, the reason why men remain emotionally and mentally weaker than women is because they are not subjected to the same hardships. That is not science—it is history and current affairs. It is exactly like when an allergen attacks your respiratory passage or a virus enters your blood system, the body might house it, feel disturbed and irritated, but with repetitive incidences, will slowly become stronger over time. The body will learn and eventually know how to fight or resist. In this same way, women become stronger as they are subjected to multiple irritants released by men and the society, over and over. Men, on the other hand, are more like the privileged kid who goes to school in a chauffeur-driven Benz and calls it hardship when the chauffeur calls in sick and he has to take public transport instead. Maybe not the fairest example, but you get the point.

Dear men, know your privileges. Anytime you think a problem for others is not a problem for you simply because it is not in your experience, is *exactly* the moment you should remind yourself that you are privileged. You are a man. That is your privilege, and you can use this privilege to make a difference when it comes to women being oppressed and discriminated against. (Don't worry, you won't run out of your privilege any time soon by using it for someone else's benefit.) Teach your sons to use theirs wisely and humanly.

CHAPTER 9

GAMES WE PLAY

THE FORD MUSTANG SHELBY (THE entire 1965–69 Shelby GT350–GT500 range) is one of my favourite cars (although what I wish to own is a Mercedes-Maybach and a Bentley—big dreams when I don't even own a bicycle in my name at the moment). My love of the car made me go watch the movie *Ford v Ferrari*. The movie enlightened me about the amazing auto race 24 Hours of Le Mans (Le Mans), run on the Circuit de la Sarthe motorsport racecourse. Besides being a well-made movie about an exceptional sport, the movie had another takeaway for me: it helped me understand a conventional marriage between a man and woman. As ridiculous as that comparison may sound, I was thrilled at finding the perfect metaphor for such a high-stakes game.

The race is a brutal test of persistence, determination, and endurance where competitors, in teams of two or three, drive illustrious marques, non-stop, over a period of twenty-four hours at speeds exceeding two hundred miles per hour. Held annually, in summer, near the town of Le Mans, France, the competition was first held in 1923. It is considered one of the most prestigious motorsport events in the world. The winner is not determined by the shortest time over a fixed distance, like in most races, but by the maximum distance covered within twenty-four hours. It's a perfect test of the vehicle's power and the team's coordination while combating any technical, strategic, or weather-related difficulties that are bound to interrupt and interfere with a team's performance. No car is inferior to any other; it is up to the team to win or lose. Drivers for each car take turns, at equal intervals, throughout the twenty-four hours so that one can rest and recover and be ready for the next set of laps. If one team member falls short during their shift, it is up to their teammate to make up for the lost time and miles, no matter the cause. This high intensity motorsport event—uniquely lengthy and full of anticipated thrills, triumphs, and unforeseen tragedies—is a prolonged adrenaline rush. The twenty-four hours are challenging for any team, and though the struggles within each team may be of differing intensity, they exist, nonetheless. Le Mans is a historic competition of high prestige which involves trying endurance and requires perfect coordination within a small team, driving and striving through a complete cycle of twenty-four hours with the only purpose of winning. Sounds like a perfect metaphor for a marriage, does it not?

However, unlike at Le Mans, the teammates in a marriage are rarely in perfectly balanced and coordinated. They seldom understand that they are both equally important in winning the race and they need to equally divide the time and work per person to win. In this conventional sport called marriage, the man is invariably perceived to be the main driver and his responsibilities are dictated by his own personal desires. The other driver, the woman, undertakes the leftover responsibilities. In the grand scheme of things, it might seem like the lead driver is doing the greater share of work by moving the car through the tracks, when in reality, it is the efforts of the second driver that constitute the majority of the labour: making up for lost time, recapturing lost miles, and recovering lost speed; filling in as a mechanic, an outrider, a trackside crew member, and even a busser.

We have already discussed, earlier in the book, the importance of teamwork and the need for division of unpaid labour at home between the two core members of this team called family. However, what gets ignored as a place of major inequity is the importance of division of leisure time between the members of the same team. As important as it is to review the unequal division of work and pay between men and women, it is also of absolute importance to address the unequal division of pleasure and comfort in patriarchal relationships and homes, the unequal division of compromises and sacrifices, and the unequal division of societal obligations: the unequal division of leisure, recreation, respite, and, indeed, happiness.

In the most accepted marriage arrangement, a married man typically and broadly follows this routine (let's call this schedule, subject to contingencies, Routine M):

- Wake up
- Eat breakfast
- Read news
- Drive to work
- Workday
- Occasional lunch with colleagues or business partners, or eat homemade lunch
- Drive back home
- Greet people in the house, rest, make *important* phone calls, etc.
- Go for a pick-up game or to the gym or to some other solo social outing that is apparently unavoidable and uninterruptable
- If not dining at home, occasionally eat dinner with friends
- Call it a day (a tough one at that)

A woman, especially a full-time working woman, follows, by default and with only a few variations, this schedule (let's call this routine, subject to contingencies, Routine W):

- Wake up, wake others in the house
- Make breakfast, eat and feed breakfast to others
- Make lunches, pack lunches (News? Who's got the time?)
- Do housework (Who else will do it?)
- *Then* go to work (driving in *some* cases)
- Workday
- Eat lunch
- Ride / Drive home
- Trip-chain on the way to buy home supplies, visit the doctor, fulfil another social duty (womanly duties before wasting time at the gym)
- Arrive home to a tired, hungry lot
- Do more housework
- If there are children, help with their schoolwork
- Cook, feed, and eat dinner
- Call it a day (the usual)

After looking at the above broadly generalized routines and seeing their stark imbalance, one would think that men have it easy and that women are enslaved with unpaid housework, whether they are homemakers or working full time. However, as true as that might be, it's not entirely the man who is responsible for this imbalance. It is the woman, in many cases, who thinks it is her job to do all of the above. Or she thinks that the tasks will be better done if she does them, rather than having to explain to someone, every day, how to do them and then have to check if the work got done at all. (In some cases, she'll have to redo the work anyway, after the poor man took four times as long to finish it in the first place.) Men, too, believe they were not made to do all that domestic work, that it is better *suited* to a woman, or they just do not see that there is *so much more work* than meets the eye in a relationship or family.

Given to a similar work routine at our house, my mother sacrificed her ties with friends and family more than my father did or had to do, all those years, because it was nearly impossible for her to indulge in any independent socializing after such a day. My father was definitely not interested in accompanying her for any excursion that did not involve his choice of people. She, however, had to accompany him everywhere, be it a personal or professional social call. He never went to an event without her if she was invited and even if she wasn't (which almost never happens in most cultures), he reluctantly fulfilled the social obligation. He never did anything recreational by himself or alone with his friends. Growing up in my house, there were never any exclusive, boys-only activities of which I knew.

Now, this situation isn't unheard of today, but is more common among my parents' generation. My close friend's parents, now that they have spent nearly four decades married, can't stand each other on most days. It's no different than with my parents. They differ in opinion just as much as they did when they were younger, maybe even more now. They may not stand each other when an old hot topic strikes up again and they fall to passionate debating until they require a referee (like all good parents need at their age). However, the very next minute, they'll get all excited about a plan to see a new movie at the theatre or to host a dinner party for common friends. Although they both have their own set of friends that they spend time with, there has to be no less than three activities together every week, planned with the same enthusiasm each time. They hate doing anything that is utterly fun without the other, and that has been their case since forever.

Today, there are more and more couples who give each other space to *do their own thing*. They are modern. In doing their own thing, the men take their much-needed space by hanging out with their male friends after work, visiting their side of the family to spend quality time with them like a dutiful son, going to the gym, or by playing a sport to burn out all the stress of adulthood and parenting. And if not any of this, then their phones take away the leftover time and energy they (genuinely) were going to spend with the wife and children, if any.

I am not sure how many women can enjoy that kind of a routine or go out to meet girlfriends every other day and not be judged or called out on it? Are there really women out there, in abundance, who go out to play a sport to burn the stress of adulthood and parenting every other evening? Do mothers put their feet up and enjoy a fine glass of bourbon after a long day at work before dinner? Going to a salon once a month or sometimes less is equal to a game of golf every Sunday, is it? There is no denying that some husbands oblige women by generously taking time off for an annual family summer vacation, believing that it compensates for women's year-long exile from me-time. Little does it matter, then, that in the end it's still the woman who ends up doing all the packing and unpacking, and everything in between, in return for this generosity.

A friend of mine in India married into another religion and experienced a lot of resentment from her family. She got married very young because that was the condition her family set for her to marry her true love: 'You cannot get married to the boy *you* choose, who is from a *different* religion, and then decide *when* you want to get married! If you want to marry him, you have to get married now.' So, she chose her love and commitment to him over dreams and ambitions of post-professional higher education. Love won. The loving husband has a very respectable job, and so does she, and they've had two adorable girls together. She falls into the typical category of a *working full-time in an office and home* kind of a mother, and the husband falls into the category of a *'Oh, I've had a long day at work, I'm going out to meet friends!'* a few times a week, kind of a hardworking man of the house. In all fairness, there is a lot of love and respect in the house. She, however, follows Routine W and he follows Routine M, and if you ask him how he likes this arrangement, I am positive he'll say he is content and a happy man. Life is great: a perfect wife, perfect kids, perfect job, perfect home, perfect routine. However, if you ask the wife how she likes the arrangement...actually, don't ask or she might start complaining (you know, *like all women do*). After all, she has everything that a *woman* could ask for, so she better be happy and content.

Another Routine W works full time at a government job (one that is hard to score for most). Her working hours are longer than her husband's due to meetings with higher state officials that last until after working hours. Being a staunch Routine M, her husband explains this situation.

'She doesn't know how to manage time or work. Other women work too, but they return in time to attend to their house duties. It isn't that difficult, really, if you try to be more responsible. It's a government job, who cares if you leave early or sit till late?'

It affects his evening schedule if she stays late at work. There was one incident where he could not make it in time for his game of squash because his wife didn't return from work, at the usual time, to take over childcare of their four-year-old daughter.

'Women tend to be careless at times,' he'd said. For many years, he had never missed that squash game for anything, not even for a funeral! 'Incompetent working wife hazards.'

He is very understanding and supportive, however, as he doesn't fight with her despite the frequent display of such shortcomings.

Another woke Routine M husband, amused with women (in this case his wife) who complain of endless body aches and are told by the doctor that the condition is stress induced, had a proclamation:

'Stress is overrated. Women just love using that as an excuse for every problem. Have you heard a man complain of stress? Men would rather play, meet friends at the field, and take care of their stress *themselves* rather than going and wasting time at the doctors or sitting with aching joints blaming stress and complaining about it all day long.'

'Alas!' I thought at that moment. 'He is right.'

Women need to learn from men to follow a strict routine, prioritize mind and body over spouse and family, and have quality me-time every day. Women need to learn to follow a disciplined lifestyle, one that is purely built on self-love, self-indulgence, and self-preservation. I am with men on this. But the mystery still remains: who will do the daily four to five hours of unpaid housework married women *have* to do, when they are out playing basketball with their girl gang every evening and going for a snack afterwards or when they are eating dinner with friends at a restaurant because the routine at home sucks?

These Routine M men are capable of spending time with their extended family, but they know, unfailingly, exactly when to get busy enough to escape not-so-exciting social obligations, especially those involving the wife's side of the family. They can escape by saying they are busy. Men are always busy. Women still have to attend all social obligations (with or without her husband), or it may look bad. Of course, how could she ever be busy enough to make excuses? The onus is on the woman of the house to keep the honour—as well as attend to family duties, nurture children, care for the elderly, and dutifully carry out the other 468 different obligations of a married couple. So, a woman definitely needs to raise her time-management game.

In all seriousness, marriage is teamwork, and unless work and responsibility is divided between the two teams equally, recreation cannot occur. At Circuit de la Sarthe, if one team member never gets a break, there is only so far the car can go in twenty-four hours. You cannot entrust the steering wheel to an overworked, exhausted team member and expect to win. It is widely researched and had been known for decades that the average lifespan of women is more than men, varying geographically across continents. There has further been plenty of research and speculation to identify reasons behind this phenomenon. I, however, would like to think it is due to all that excess physical and mental labour that women are put through, which ends up making them tougher and, as a result, they live longer than men, who have been coddled. Longer lifespan, however, does not necessarily mean an ailment free life. Given this overloaded, no-break lifestyle, women end up suffering stress-related ailments, which can worsen other health issues that might be a result of age or ill-fate. Women's hormones are never their best friends, and the relationship keeps getting worse with age, causing additional limitations and discomforts. The systems of society—which load guilt on women, by default, every time they do something self-gratifying—are well rooted in all of us. Apparently, there is so much more a woman could have done (out of that list of 468 things to do) instead of indulging in her so-called me-time. Clearly, she caused inconvenience to her family.

I was pleasantly surprised (loved it, actually) when Caroline Criado Perez, pointed to recent research 'that has emerged showing that while women tend to assess their intelligence accurately, men of average intelligence think they are more intelligent than two-thirds of people.' It is exactly this illusion that results in more confidence among men who consider themselves superior, and therefore, tend to either outperform themselves or underrate the abilities of other genders. In the case of these men, outperforming oneself is fairly undemanding since their original capacity is (understandably) lesser than that of women. Going by the research and other established evidences from my daily life that point out the same facts, I believe women should not try to be equal to men. Women should not accept the normal for men to be the absolute normal for them, too. Instead, men should try to live and achieve an equal status to women. Men should realign their normalcy compass to the absolute normal for women because women *do* assess things more accurately. This realignment might help bring equilibrium into being.

In response to every claim made in this book, there will be a few readers thinking, 'That doesn't happen in my house,' or 'I don't do that,' or 'I have never seen this happen.' If some behaviour or situation doesn't happen in a home or a neighbourhood, it does not mean that such situations and behaviours don't exist. If you are someone who is as knowledgeable or sensitive towards gender bias, you can certainly contribute to eliminating it.

There are women who consider housework to be their coveted field, their reigning seat of honour. They do not want to give up the special status and privileges attached to being the lady of the house or the supermom, however much they exhaust themselves while managing a house, a family, and a job. They take pride in childcare and rightly so. But their pride is so strong that they convince themselves childcare is not a man's job and, once again, rob a man of an opportunity for pleasure and responsibility that they might, on the contrary, cherish if given a taste of.

This is a vicious cycle of inequality created by women themselves that can only be corrected by changing the things to which women attach feelings of fulfilment. Men are not bad at childcare, neither are they bad at managing a house or running errands and cooking for the family on a daily basis. Our biological configurations do not lend us corresponding skill sets. It is all about adapting to personal needs over desires. Any human being, when subjected to a situation that demands attention, care, and action, will naturally develop the skills for it, if not known or learned before. Moreover, practise makes perfect, so let the man practise doing half the unpaid housework while the woman goes golfing!

Women need to relinquish the pride attached to such things that contradict their own demand for gender equality. We are confusing men with such contradictions, giving them an opportunity to justify and practise sexism. Men may not be as intelligent as they think themselves to be or as they seem to be, so why not clear up the superiority misconceptions and cut down on such performance pressure for them. Spell it out loud and clear what men need to do to help women get the me-time they yearn for. They need to be reminded that women, too, need time to breath between laps on Le Circuit, so the team can make the most of the available twenty-four hours and succeed in this game of two.

Unsolicited Suggestion #9

I recently read somewhere on a social media platform that a person's greatest contribution to the world may not be something they do but who they raise, and that is exactly why whatever you do today is going to shape the society you create by raising children. It is known that children learn from their parents' actions more than their words. My dear men, show your sons that you value their mother's time as much as you value your own. Show your children you value her efforts and understand that, inevitably, she has to do more than you will ever need to. I don't mean to sound like a charlatan claiming to be an expert in human behaviour or psychology, but I do know these small practices can make an enormous difference to the cause of equality.

Do not help your wives in the kitchen or with other housework and expect rewards for taking thirty minutes off her weekly unpaid job at home. If you do not thank her eight times for every time she manages in your absence, do not expect words of appreciation from her after cooking a Sunday lunch while she took her much-deserved break. Ask yourself, at that time, that if there was a penny for every minute you got to spend on yourself *because* your wife at home was managing the fort, how many rooms full of pennies would that be? Reward motivates everyone, for sure, so she needs appreciation and reward as much as you do. Reward your wife daily for all the work she does on your behalf or just do the work yourself because it is also *your* work to do.

If she forgets to do something because she got busy elsewhere or because she was out taking a break, don't guilt trip her. That is emotional abuse. Do that work yourself. Show your children that whatever a mom can do, a dad can do as well. Do not bring up that you 'had to do it the other day, too' every time you have to fill in for your wife. Do not tell your wife you sacrificed your evening for her work, that you could have spent that time at the gym instead. Everything at home that you consider to be your wife's work is your work too, so just find more time for her the same way that you find more time for yourself, repeatedly, without failing.

Moreover, childcare is not only a woman's job. bell hooks again very rightly pointed out how even the most equalist couples become unequal after childbirth because it is presumably only the mother's job to take care of and raise children. Couples need to work hard to maintain equity in this sphere as much as in any other, and most men choose to not work hard towards it because they think they are already working hard enough at their paid jobs. Men, don't just spend *quality time* with your children (when it suits your schedule) because you love them. Take charge of them, equally, because they are *your* children, too.

Dear men, do not generalize and make comments like 'women always complain', 'women gossip too much', or 'women are supposed to do this', especially when you are a parent. First, women complain because of all the extra work, extra stress, extra health issues, and lack of team spirit, or even compassion, that they have to deal with. I cannot stress this point enough. Second, men gossip equally if not more than women; although, it's no myth that men are worse than women at keeping secrets. Men spend more time gossiping at work than women do. Men also spend more time outside the house in gossip-enabling recreation and leisure indulgence. They talk on the phone for longer than women have the time for, either at home or at work. A man might call it a work call or an important discussion, but we all know it's mostly gossip. Men waste more time gossiping than the time women only wish they had for gossiping. Women might not complain as much if they could participate in all such recreational activities, too.

Kate Manne makes this fascinating observation:

> Women may not be simply human *beings* but positioned as human *givers* when it comes to the dominant men who look to them for various kinds of moral support, admiration, attention, and so on. She is not allowed to *be* in the same ways as he is. She will tend to be in trouble when she does not give enough, or to the right people, in the right way, or in the right spirit. And, if she errs on this score, or asks for something of the same support or attention on her own behalf, there is a risk of misogynist resentment, punishment, and indignation.
>
> So a woman's recognized humanity may leave much to be desired by way of moral freedom. And her sense of obligation is then likely to be excessive, on the one hand, and lacking, in many others.

Men, don't fret, fuss, or ignore women when they fall sick too often, instead, understand that their needs are different and more complex and to top it, they get no time to rest and recharge without constant guilt trips. The least you can do is to not dismiss or mock women's complaints. Set better examples, especially if you are raising other human beings who are definitely observing you.

I wish for women, too, to not accept such imbalance and understand how it is negatively affecting society at large. Do not accept unequal relief from duties and call it adjustment. Do not say 'I chose this to maintain peace in my marriage,' or 'I chose it. Period.' When you choose inequality, you feed inequality to future generations. Make a decision to choose self-respect and self-worth over a social display of false contentment in honour of herd mentality.

There are women and books who also blame feminism for all the troubles women have to go through because of the whole idea of feminism, but is that really true? Feminism was never about fighting with men but about women knowing their rights. It's about self-love, self-awareness, self-esteem, and self-actualization. It's about knowing that we as women deserve respect, and it's about men knowing that they need to respect us. Respect could be for a choice to bear children or not and opting for motherhood, or it could be for staying childless and following ambitions, or for wanting both and seeking positive support from a partner to achieve it. Respect her choice and her time the same way she respects yours.

Marriage is about *playing fair* to triumph at this high-endurance, twenty-four-hour sport for two that lasts a lifetime. Dear men, be a sport!

CHAPTER 10

EN FIN

*It's difficult to see the glass ceiling because it's made of glass.
Virtually invisible. What we need is for more birds to fly above it
and shit all over it, so we can see it properly.*

—Caitlin Moran, *How to Be a Woman*

IT *IS* DIFFICULT TO SEE the glass ceiling because it is clear glass,
but many women over hundreds of years have tried to shatter
that glass with bold steps and bolder voices. But the ceiling is
still unshattered. The fact that some say it isn't there, that there
is equality, is because there have not been enough cracks in the
glass that could make it more visible to the naked eye. Wouldn't
it be interesting if we could make this glass ceiling a skylight
instead? Or we could roll it back like a sunroof!

We find it easier to criticize the idea and movement of
feminism today because there were women who fought for
freedom of expression, the right to vote, and freedom to choose
for women. I am able to write a book today because of those
women, who gave up their entire life to make an egalitarian
society, a society where everyone has the right to education and
freedom of speech. It is these women who paved the way for
the privileges that we as women enjoy today. And that is exactly
what makes it easy for some of us to condemn something
that we neither had to suffer to achieve nor struggle to secure

in our lifetimes. Even though we enjoy more privileges than the women before us did, women are still not free or equal and neither can we be unless we recognize the biases that are nevertheless embossed in our society.

As women, we participate in patriarchy, all of us do, by perpetuating strict gender roles, that tell us equality does more harm than good, that preach inequality to children even before they are born. We justify this unequal mindset by calling it tradition, culture, or even religion. No tradition, culture, or religion can be good if it teaches dominance. Moreover, many religious and non-religious historic texts were written by men of the times (since women had few rights and definitely not the freedom to write), so there was no other way to have it written than to make it sound like men were of paramount importance and intelligence compared to women and were, therefore, unimpeachable. If I was writing philosophical doctrine, I would glorify myself too, wouldn't you?

How I see it, going back a few centuries, society followed a more gender equal narrative in a lot of ways. There are various texts and stories with numerous translations and more than a few contrasting interpretations and viewpoints for each; nonetheless, those narrations still date back to a thousand years ago. In my view, whoever wrote them emphasized, intentionally or unintentionally, certain things that suggest that women inhabited a different role than what it has become in the last few hundred years. For example, in Indian epics which describe societies from nearly ten thousand years ago (that presumably form the bedrock of many of the cultures of the Indian subcontinent), warrior sons were known by their mother's names and not by their father's: Kunti Putra meaning the Sons of Kunti, Devaki Nandan for Lord Krishna meaning Devaki's Son, Anjani Putra for Lord Hanuman meaning Anjana's Son, etc. Daughters were named after their fathers, who were Kings, or after the kingdom itself: Gandhari, the Princess of Gandhar Kingdom; Janaki, the daughter of King Janak was also called Maithili after her kingdom of Mithila; Draupadi, the daughter of King Drupad. There are plenty of other prominent women who evidently echo strength, courage, and wisdom in more than a few events throughout Indian scriptures and stories. In fact, that was how I got my name. It was derived from my father's name, him hoping his daughter might become great like those women in ancient texts (but alas!). There are Indian goddesses who are considered as powerful as and worshipped equally as their male counterparts. What we took away from all these portrayals of women is not very clear today.

I do not completely blame men for being insensitive, but their insensitivity is not just because women are equally responsible for this twisted lifestyle that we are all living today. I believe, in part, that they lack sensitivity because it is not easy to understand, relate to, or even be aware of these deeply rooted inequalities of our everyday lives without having been subjected to them. It took me twenty-four years and a displacement from India to America to realize that what my mother did for her children was not normal. The first time I had to cook for myself and manage my own home is when I first realized how gargantuan that task was and how much we took it for granted as kids when we were being fed by our parents. The second time it hit me (and this had a much bigger impact) was when I got married at twenty-eight only to further realize how unequal society at large and the world in general are. I was raised in a protected, atypical environment, among only one kind of people and believed that that milieu was all that the world had to offer and there was nothing left to see. Despite being in one of the world's most populated countries, my own everyday world—an entire city—did not comprise 0.01 per cent of the real world outside.

For twenty-eight years, I did not know that the things my mother (indeed, any mother) did for us, every single day, with a big broad smile despite having a patriarchal husband (who at least helped out at home), were extraordinarily formidable in quantity and nature. Unless men do *all* of what women have to do, there is no way on earth that they can naturally understand how complex and gruelling the demands are or what women go through in the process of meeting them. Since it is, evidently, nearly impossible for men to understand women's struggles completely (it doesn't help that on top of that they overestimate their intelligence!) and to understand how women are more enduring than them, all that is expected of men, in the struggle for gender equality, is to at least consider women equal.

There are men who try to understand women's struggles and there are men who don't. Then there are men who pull down other men who want to be feminist or practise equality. Most men today believe in equality only as long as they are not inconvenienced by it or are not being shamed for it. When they have more people around them who mock their belief in feminism than those who take pride in it, these feminists give up inside. I call them subconscious misogynists. I wish men were not so weak at holding their ground on this subject. I wish men who did not believe in, or practise equality, would be embarrassed and ashamed instead. I also wish more women strove to understand feminism and were willing to believe openly in equality. Maybe it is the misconstrued idea of feminism as a fight against men (an ignorant perception) that discourages some women? Maybe it is the fact that women have always been forced to follow since time immemorial (and men have been forced to lead). Perhaps they find comfort in the known.

Maybe the idea of overturning the power asymmetry seems threatening to the dominant and, therefore, unsettling to the dominated. Consequently, men and women are prevented from accepting gender equality.

Women alone cannot fight this social disunity, caused by the ignorance of one specific gender. False beliefs and pernicious ideologies concocted by emotionally debilitated individuals is what makes a civilization backward. Oppression in any form, be it direct, indirect, accepted, unaccepted, ultimately results in rage among the oppressed, and when the oppressed attempt to speak out, it is this rage that manifests itself. It is the same reason why in the case of gender equality and the strike against patriarchy, feminism has been misunderstood.

Rage has not helped abolish sexism. It has made people resent feminism instead. Today, Millennials and Generation Z members speak more openly than before for gender equality. Yet, some speak against it, as I observed during debates in formal or informal social settings. The ones resenting the concept and speaking against it are mostly those with little knowledge of the history of feminism. They are unwilling to comprehend that feminism isn't about 'who's better than whom' or about putting one down to raise the other up, their ignorance highly exacerbated by a lack of experience in the world outside of their social circle, institutes, or communities in most cases. This reverses the efforts of a hundred-odd years and of a million women in the past. Many of us do not understand that the reason we can flagrantly debate on this subject today is because women before us have raised their voices and because women have struggled to be treated like humans. Misinformation and negative sentiments about feminism negate the struggles of a million sufferers who selflessly gave their lives for gender equality. Not only did they liberate women through their sacrifices, but they made it possible for anyone to proudly say, 'But not all men.' Not all men are sexist today *because* women started this movement for equality in the first place. Not all men are sexist and not all women are feminists, and that is what makes conversations about feminism mandatory.

Men do not have to be feminine to be feminists. Alternative masculinity can be a conscious choice for men. It can be a choice that does not threaten their glorified persona, glorified by themselves and twice as much by women. Women do not have to be man-haters to be feminists. Misconstruing feminism is a way to deflect attention away from the actual cause. All I wish is for everyone to understand the real reasons and purpose of feminism and for feminism to reclaim its definition and reflect its true intentions: abolition of sexism and promotion of humanitarianism. Or, in the words of my very favourite, Gloria Steinem, 'A feminist is anyone who recognizes the equality and full humanity of women and men.' Plain and simple!

I chose not to discuss serious crimes against women—like domestic violence, physical abuse, mental abuse, sexual harassment, and rape—because these cannot be done justice in simple discussions, nor are they a hidden truth in any way for anyone. I chose to discuss these other issues, however unimportant or non-existent they may seem, because they still consume a very large part of a woman's life every day. These seem like they make an iota of a difference but for most they make up for an entire life story. If these quotidian discriminations can affect a human being so gravely, imagine the damage done by violence.

I do further believe that feminist men and women alone cannot change the patriarchal mindset unless the collective mindset of families changes. An egalitarian family can make for a fair and just egalitarian society. Unless one family at a time evolves and practises gender equality, the struggles of inequality for women will not end socially. It took an extended, subconscious effort by an old-school, rigid father and an egalitarian mother to easily (they won't like the choice of easily here) raise three feminist children in a dysfunctional Indian family. My parents' efforts clearly prove that raising feminist children isn't that hard a task to achieve. Parents just need to decide to do so and then do it a little more consciously.

My father, with three siblings, was raised by a single mother who also managed her deceased husband's businesses in the fifties and the sixties. This often makes me wonder why he still turned out to be such a proud sexist! Maybe he projects that emotion more as an attempt to fit in to the rest of the sexist world around him that embarrasses his inner self. He has acquired and inherited a fair amount of intolerable misogynistic views from the society he grew up in and the one he tries to fit in now. Those stand out so loud and clear that I think if it wasn't for the three children, as living examples of his inner beliefs, there would be no way anyone could ever find out he was a feminist at heart. It's complex!

Who you raise, is what really matters in the end. Raise a feminist family and hope that others do too. Wouldn't a feminist world be a great world for your own children to live in? What we are missing today is the equality that allows men to express emotions and accept failures, that keeps women from being called the B word because they have an opinion and are in control, eliminating their internalized sexism as much as external sexism and misogyny.

Srikhand would often tell me, 'Don't just talk about the problems, discuss their solutions.' That concept helped me a lot. It is that same approach that made me want to discuss the problem of sexism and gender inequality (common to all), which

I cannot get myself to overlook. Therefore, I decided to take my compassion a step further and lay out possible solutions to these issues and share them with you. It is my hope that we can all follow them, collectively, to truly achieve a renaissance of equality in the twenty-first century.

The solution is quite simple. Let us all raise feminist families.

ACKNOWLEDGEMENTS

The list of people who have helped me reach this point where I can write an acknowledgement section is a long one; I may never be able to do justice to it. These aren't just people who helped me during my writing and publishing journey, but numerous others who have helped me, by allowing me to be the way I wished to be for however long I wanted, and accepting me as I was. As clichéd as it may sound, I cannot thank my friends and family enough for their constant faith in me and the support they give me in everything I do (and trust me, I do a lot of things that constantly leave them baffled). Thank YOU!

I love you all—Mummy, Papa, Kanu Di, and Shashaank. As dysfunctional, and as crazy and dramatic as we are, I would never trade you for another family. Thank you for adding Greg and Smriti to this family, who are as crazy as the rest of us so it feels like they have been family forever. Thank you, all of you, for watching out for me and having my back always. Especially Mummy—you have been an unfailingly loyal advocate (a silent but effective one) and a stalwart supporter giving me my space while I was tumbling from multiple transitions from being an architect to an author and everything in between. Papa, thank you for forcibly depositing money in my account at such times, even when I didn't ask. I am sure to always be fine with a family like mine!

I cannot thank my girlfriends enough, all the 'powerpuffed', independent women who have constantly been my strength, no matter the distance, and an inspiration to everyone around them. You are my extended family, loving and supporting me as my family has, and I am extremely privileged to have you in my life.

This book in particular stands on some very strong shoulders that I want to thank specifically. The first one would have to be Smriti, for that video call to cheer me up when I was all bummed with being stuck in America during a lockdown and with a herniated disc. You lit a magical spark that started with a frenzied twenty-four-hour writing marathon and eventually this book. Oh! And that magic and spark would have been for naught had it not been for Shashaank forcing me to switch from my ten-year-old laptop to a fancy new MacBook with keys that tempted me to keep typing for hours despite the turmoil and uncertainty of being stuck with a bad back in another country during a pandemic. Thanks to that new laptop, Shashaank, all the thoughts racing through my head during those long days and nights that I was bedridden (floor-ridden actually as the beds in America were too soft for my poor back) were streamlined into writing this book. You made that possible with your usual thoughtful, practical, attentive, and selfless ability to take care of your loved ones that stuns us all. Thank you, Greg, for putting up with me in your beautiful house for those intense months when I hijacked half your home and made it my own writing den; for having patience for my quirks while being locked in the same house the whole time, while I disconnected from the world to write and then walked around the house like a ghost when you needed to sleep. Thank you, Kanu Di, for feeding me those sourdough turkey sandwiches for lunches (I still crave them) and the fresh hot meals every evening, while all I did was eat, sleep, breathe, and write. You kept me feeling all taken care of and are a large part of this book reaching fruition. Your ceaseless love and attention—from meals and girl time to proofreading letters and early drafts—became a pillar I could lean against while I focused on writing. All of you and the book made me forget how physically incapacitated I was throughout that time and helped me heal better than any rehabilitation could.

Jaimee Garbacik from Footnote Editorial and Daniel Heila: thank you for being my first copy editors. Daniel, your funny add-ons to the editorial notes kept me awake and kicking while tackling our tight editing schedule. You both made my manuscript look crisp before I could take it to my literary agent, Kanishka Gupta at Writer's Side, and make an impression. Thank you Kanishka for being as excited about the book as I was right from the first time I introduced it to you. Neelini Sarkar and you were extremely helpful in further refining the book and for believing in it as much as I did. Thank you also to my editorial team at Aleph for working on the book consistently with me and answering all my first-time-author questions with patience and without judgement.

It would be only fair to thank life for teaching me all the lessons I needed to learn to write this book. Life, buddy, you are working too hard on me though. Thank you for that, but it won't kill you to take a break once in a while and let me breathe too.

Last but not least: Aadya and Siddhant, you may have done nothing to make this book come to life but you still rank as #1 heart stealers for me!

Abhari

NOTES AND REFERENCES

47 Interestingly, World Bank's research shows that women are invariably more likely than men to walk or take public transport: 'Global Mobility Report 2017', Sustainable Mobility for All, available at https://openknowledge.worldbank.org/bitstream/handle/10986/28542/120500.pdf?sequence=6.

47 In France, two thirds of public transport passengers are women: Caroline Criado Perez, *Invisible Women: Exposing Data Bias in a World Designed for Men*, New York: Abrams Press, 2019, pp. 29–30.

48 Women do 75% of the world's unpaid care work: Ibid., p. 30.

67 We know that just employment and education do not liberate women from male domination: C. S. Stamarski and L. S. Son Hing, 'Gender inequalities in the workplace: the effects of organizational structures, processes, practices, and decision makers' sexism', *Frontiers in Psychology*, Vol. 6, Issue 1400, 2015.

67 'There are many high-paid professional women': bell hooks, *Feminism Is for Everybody: Passionate Politics*, Boston: South End Press, 2000, p. 49.

76 For most of these acts, there is hardly a way to prove that it happened: 'Why stalking is rampant in India despite a strict law', *Hindustan Times*, 10 July 2017; Mehak Dhiman, 'High Rate of Acquittal in Rape Cases: Cause and Concern', *LatestLaws.com*, 27 August 2021.

84 'Doubt is the greatest gift we can give to each other': Ali Sina, 'Why I Left Islam: My Passage From Faith to Enlightenment', Ibn Warraq (ed.), *Leaving Islam: Apostates Speak Out*, New York: Prometheus Books, 2003, pp. 149–50.

93 '50/50 division of floor space has even been formalized in plumbing codes': Perez, *Invisible Women*, p. 48.

95   There is a lot of talk (and mostly just talk) about the dearth of toilets in rural areas: Sarita Vijay Panchang, Pratima Joshi & Smita Kale, 'Women "holding it" in urban India: Toilet avoidance as an under-recognized health outcome of sanitation insecurity', *Global Public Health*, 2021, p. 3.

95   a phenomenon termed as 'toilet avoidance': Ibid., p. 10.

96   '[In] December 2014, Bombay's high court ordered all municipal corporations': Perez, *Invisible Women*, p. 51.

113   'Most notably, in a review of forty-five studies on leadership and gender': Tomas Chamorro-Premuzic, *Why Do So Many Incompetent Men Become Leaders? (and how to fix it)*, Boston: Harvard Business Review Press, 2019, p. 9.

137   It is widely researched and had been known for decades that the average lifespan of women is more than men: Robert H. Shmerling, 'Why men often die earlier than women', *Harvard Health Blog*, 22 June 2020.

138   'that has emerged showing that while women tend to assess their intelligence accurately': Perez, *Invisible Women*, p. 108.

141   Second, men gossip equally if not more than women: Ginka Toegel, '"Women talk too much" simply isn't true, data show', IMD, February 2021; 'Overturn stereotypes: Men gossip more than women', *Economic Times*, 17 February 2014.

142   'Women may not be simply human *beings* but positioned as human *givers*': Kate Manne, *Down Girl: The Logic of Misogyny*, Oxford: Oxford University Press, 2017, p. xxi.

145   nonetheless, those narrations still date back to a thousand years ago: Anindita Basu, 'Mahabharata', *World History Encyclopedia*, 25 August 2016.

149   'A feminist is anyone who recognizes the equality and full humanity of women and men': Gloria Steinem, cited in Jill Robinson, Maura Harrington, Chris Cartwright, and Kevin Walsh, 'Connective Leadership: From Zero-Sum to Inclusion', *Breaking the Zero-Sum Game: Transforming Societies Through Inclusive Leadership*, 2017, Bingley: Emerald Publishing, p. 209.

FURTHER READING

Adichie, Chimamanda Ngozi, *Dear Ijeawele, or A Feminist Manifesto in Fifteen Suggestions*, New York: Knopf Publishers, 2017.

Chamorro-Premuzic, Tomas, *Why Do So Many Incompetent Men Become Leaders? (and how to fix it)*, Boston: Harvard Business Review Press, 2019.

hooks, bell, *Feminism Is for Everybody: Passionate Politics*, Boston: South End Press, 2000.

Manne, Kate, *Down Girl: The Logic of Misogyny*, Oxford: Oxford University Press, 2017.

Moran, Caitlin, *How to Be a Woman*, London: Ebury Press, 2011.

Perez, Caroline Criado, *Invisible Women: Exposing Data Bias in a World Designed for Men*, New York: Abrams Press, 2019.

Sina, Ali, 'Why I Left Islam: My Passage From Faith to Enlightenment', Ibn Warraq (ed.), *Leaving Islam: Apostates Speak Out*, New York: Prometheus Books, 2003.

West, Lindy, *Shrill: Notes from a Loud Woman*, New York: Hachette Books, 2017.